Reason & Rationality in the Quran

Reason & Rationality in the Quran

Ibrahim Kalin

CLARITAS
BOOKS

1 2 3 4 5 6 7 8 9 10

CLARITAS BOOKS

Bernard Street, Swansea, United Kingdom
Milpitas, California, United States

CLARITAS
BOOKS

First Published in April 2018

Typeset in Minion Pro 14/11
Printed by Mega Printing in Turkey

Reason & Rationality in The Quran
by Ibrahim Kalin

A CIP catalogue record for this book is available from the British Library

ISBN: 978-1-905837-51-9

بسم الله الرحمن الرحيم

CONTENTS

IBRAHIM KALIN is the Spokesperson for the President of the Republic of Turkey and Deputy Secretary-General of Presidency of the Republic of Turkey. He served as Assistant Undersecretary of State and Senior Advisor to the Prime Minister of Turkey before taking up his current post. Dr. Kalin is the founding-director of the SETA Foundation for Political, Economic and Social Research based in Ankara, Turkey and served as its director from 2005 to 2009. A graduate of Istanbul University, he received his M.A. from ISTAC, International Islamic University of Malaysia and Ph.D. from George Washington University. As a broadly trained scholar of philosophy and Islamic studies, he has taught courses on Islamic philosophy, comparative philosophy, Islam-West relations and Turkish foreign policy. His academic and intellectual work focuses on the Islamic intellectual tradition and its relevance for the contemporary world. He is the editor-in-chief of the 2-Volume Oxford Encyclopedia of Philosophy, Science and Technology in Islam (Oxford University Press, 2014). Dr. Kalin is also the co-editor together with John Esposito of Islamophobia and the Challenge of Pluralism in the 21st Century, (Oxford University Press, 2011).

INTRODUCTION

This book is based on a simple argument: far from being a self-standing entity, reason functions within a larger context of existence, intelligibility and moral thinking. It articulates as much as discloses the reality of things. Rationality arises within a context of meaning and significance that goes beyond the internal workings of the individual human mind. As a situated and engaged reality, reason by itself is neither a principle nor ground of knowledge, truth or rationality because our epistemic encounter with the world takes place in a wider context of ontological relations and significance. Furthermore, the conceptual and linguistic affiliates of the word *ʿaql*, which make up a long list of interrelated epistemic terms, present a matrix of thinking wider than calculative and discursive rationality can account for. The Quran treats reason and rationality in such a wider context of thinking.

Any notion of rationality that can properly be called 'Islamic' operates in the context of what I call the metaphysics of creation, which states that the world has been created by an intelligent God for a purpose. It begins with the premise that the world has a beginning and an end and that *all shall perish except His [God's] Face* (Al-Qasas, 28:88). The beginning (*al-mabda'*) and the end or "return" (*al-ma'ad*) to God lays out a scope and horizon for our rational deliberations and moral choices. Like the universe, human beings have been created for a purpose whose fulfillment is not possible within the confines of a subjectivist ontology of human reason. The work of reason takes place against the backdrop of an ontology of rationality that links human beings to other human beings on the one hand, and to God and the universe on the other.

As God's intelligent work, the world of creation reflects His creative power. Given that God creates optimally and always for a purpose, the universe has an order and intelligibility built into it. Truth, when properly accessed, is the 'disclosure' of this intrinsic order and intelligibility, which God as the Creator has bestowed upon existence. When reason investigates natural phenomena and the universe, it seeks out this order and intelligibility in them because without order, structure and intelligibility we cannot know anything. To name something, without which we cannot perceive the world, means giving it a proper place and signification in the order of things. A non-subjectivist ontology of reason, which the Quran advocates, construes rationality as disclosing the principles of intelligibility derived from the intrinsic qualities of the order of existence. 'Rationality as intelligibility' is thus markedly different from the current notions of instrumental rationality, which reduces the function of reason, the most fundamental trait of being human, to making logical use of available means to reach our stated ends.[1]

Rationality is then a function of existence and thinking and takes place in a communicative and intersubjective context. To say that something is intelligible means that it has a certain order and structure by which we can understand it. It also means that since it is intelligible, it can be communicated to others through language and rational arguments. This intersubjective context of rationality, which the Quran emphasizes on various occasions, places reason and rationality above the solitary work of a solipsistic and disengaged mind. Just as we humans are part of a larger reality, our thinking functions within a larger context of intelligibility. Using the plural form, the Quran explains its verses to a tribe, nation or community (qawm) who thinks and chastises those who do not use their reason (see for instance, Al-Baqarah, 2:164; Al-Ma'idah, 5:58; Al-Ra'd, 13:4; Al-Nahl, 16:12). From disclosing the intrinsic intelligibility of things to intercultural relations, rationality emerges in a network of relations and connections that go beyond the internal procedures of the human mind.

Subsuming reason within a larger context of existence goes against the main thrust of modern rationalism. Ever since the European Enlightenment adapted its 'baptism of reason' against the alleged irrationality of the Middle Ages, reason has declared its independence and developed a view of itself as the ultimate *arche* and *ens realissimum* of reality. In an age in which rationality is measured by quantifiable properties and computerised decisions, the ontological foundations of reason have radically changed, and highly idealised and eventually inhuman forms of rationality have been identified as the basis of human intelligence. In contrast to the notion of rationality as computerisation, however, our most unique human quality called reason, the very quality that distinguishes us from the rest of creation and clearly privileges us over them (Al-Isra', 17:70), functions essentially and primarily in a qualitative and axiological context. Charges of 'irrationality' and dogmatism have been launched against Islam in part because the concept of rationality as developed in the Islamic intellectual tradition contravenes the main thrust of modern and postmodern notions of rationality that have arisen in the West since the 17th and 18th centuries.

Motivated by religious zeal, most medieval Christians considered Islam to be against reason and saw it as grounded in blind faith, ignorance, violence and worldly pleasures. The Muslim faith attracted many followers, it was argued, not because it offered convincing arguments but because it appealed to their flesh, the lowest part of the human being. Furthermore, Islam endorsed violence on non-Muslims to convert them because it could not have produced rational arguments to convince the non-believer. Use of violence and declaration of jihad against non-Muslims showed how irrational Islam was and how Islamic faith went against the nature of things. Not surprisingly, charges of unreason and violence have survived to the modern period. Today, radically anti-Islamic and Islamophobic voices cite similar arguments to depict Islam and Muslims as irrational and violent. History, though, has its own acts of balancing. Some medieval critics of Christianity such as Peter Bayle and Henry Stubbe defended Islam as a faith closer to reason than the Catholic Church. They praised the simplicity of Islamic faith against the complexities of Christian theology and rituals and admired the advanced state of Islamic civilisation. While people like Roger Bacon claimed that the Muslim philosophers al-Farabi and Ibn Sina had produced their philosophical edifice despite Islam, not because of it, and pretended to be Muslims outwardly to avoid the persecution of an intolerant religion, the anti-Catholic thinkers of the Middle Ages believed that Islam tolerated rational thinking and scientific inquiry more than others.[2]

The secular critics consider Islam as essentially incompatible with the secular-humanist ethos of modernity and thus in conflict with the supposedly rational-scientific basis of modern culture. They also point to the discrepancies between traditional religions and the modern concepts of human rights, equality and freedom. The Enlightenment reason claims autonomy and self-sufficiency and rejects any outside authority such as history, tradition or religion. It does not reject religion in toto but subjects it to the scrutiny of the individual human reason. It draws boundaries for religious belief and denies any role or authority to religion outside them.

Like the medieval critics, the secular critics of Islam link unreason and violence and allege that "Islamic terrorism" is a result of the irrational nature of the Islamic faith. The radical Orientalists add other things to the list: the oppression of women, violation of minority rights, freedom of press, even poverty, corruption etc., are all somehow related to the Islamic tradition which did not allow free thinking and oppressed free inquiry, dissent and pluralism. Needless to say, this is a caricature of the Islamic tradition and based on political considerations rather than a sound analysis of historical facts. Much of the current debate about Islam, reason, rationality and science in popular circles in the West is shaped by such simplistic yet powerful views.

The Modern Context: The Enlightenment Reason

Modernity via the Enlightenment has claimed superiority over other traditions and non-Western cultures because of its claim to ground things in reason and thus create a primarily, if not purely, rational order. In contrast to the supposedly fideistic claims of Christianity, the Enlightenment philosophers sought to justify everything on the basis of what Descartes called "clear and distinct ideas". The question to which Kant responded with his famous essay in 1784 summed up the relevance of reason and rationality for how we were to live in the post-Medieval world: do we live in an enlightened age? Kant believed his generation lived in an "age of enlightenment" rather than in an "enlightened age". The subtle difference between the two is not to be taken lightly. An enlightened age is one in which the defining elements of culture, society and politics follow the principle of reason. This is presumably a mature state of humanism and rationality, a world in which reason has defeated the forces of anti-reason. By contrast, an age of enlightenment is one in which the battle for the soul of humanity continues and the forces of reason fight ignorance and darkness. It refers to a process of gradual maturity and rationality, a goal towards which humanity as a whole moves. Since the reign of reason has begun, the end of history is within our reach – an end that is certain to come when the light of reason dawns upon all humanity including non-Europeans.

Kant defined enlightenment as "man's release from his self-incurred tutelage. Tutelage is man's inability to make use of his understanding without direction from another". Man's immaturity has created much of the oppression and ignorance that has shaped human history. Kant characterises the essence of the Enlightenment as the "courage to think" for oneself freely. "Sapere aude! Have courage to use your own reason! That's the motto of enlightenment".[3]

From academic circles to populist politics, the debate about the Enlightenment reason has now become a debate about the alleged lack of rationality and humanity in Islam. In his preface to his brilliant history of the Enlightenment, Louis Dupre, "stunned by the attacks on September 11, 2001", wondered "if there was any purpose in writing about the Enlightenment at a time that so brutally seemed to announce the end of its values and ideals". Dupre does not mean to declare Islamic culture "unenlightened". But he notes that "Islam never had to go through a prolonged period of critically examining the validity of its spiritual vision, as the West did during the eighteenth century".[4] Dupre does not explain why Islam needs to revisit the "validity of its spiritual vision" but he clearly echoes an increasingly common view about the so-called "Islamic reformation". There have been other more alarming voices calling for an 'Islamic enlightenment' to save Muslims from backwardness and the world from an irrational and dangerous religion.

It is a common mistake to assume that reason has been the exclusive property of the Enlightenment thinking since the 18th century. Traditional societies have accorded reason an important place in theology, law, politics, ethics, art and other areas of human life. The Islamic intellectual tradition, for instance, has produced an immense literature on reason, rationality, logic, thinking, contemplation, scientific inquiry, and so on. From Sunni and Shi'ite theology to Peripatetic philosophy and Sufism, the classical works are filled with chapters on the nobility of reason, virtues of knowledge and the spiritual blessings of using one's reason properly. The notions of reason and rationality that have developed in this tradition, however, are radically different from their modern counterparts. Traditional societies have seen reason as part of a larger reality and placed them within the wider context of existence and meaning. In order to function properly, reason has to accept its place within an order of things that is larger than the knowing subject. As I shall discuss below, the Quran considers human reason as part of a larger reality whose meaning cannot be encapsulated and disclosed by logical analysis, conceptual abstraction or rational discourse alone. The timeless wisdom is that reality is always more than our epistemic constructions of it.

As a mark of modernity, reason has been constructed as a self-regulating principle and the arbiter of truth from the mathematical and physical sciences to social and political orders. One modern tribute to it reads as follows: "The virtue of rationality means the recognition and acceptance of reason as one's only source of knowledge, one's only judge of values and one's only guide to action."[5] But in reality, this rarefied view of reason, so passionately defended by academic philosophers, positivists and the self-proclaimed Enlightenment rationalists, has never worked as expected. Nor has it delivered what it promised i.e., free individuals, rational society, universal equality, scientific culture, reason-bound politics or economic justice. This in itself calls for a deep reflection about the reasonableness of the Enlightenment project of pure reason. At any rate, elements of 'anti-reason' seem to have crept into the new world order promised by the Enlightenment, and the modern capitalist society with its evasive impersonalism, crude individualism and structural violence, is a far cry from a rational social order.

Ever since the triumph of scientism in the late 19th and early 20th century, reason as logic and rational inquiry has been hailed as a trait of modernity not because we want to grasp the reality of things in the Greek sense of the term but because a purely rational order is believed to enable us to have full control over the world. The instrumental rationality that defines our value schemes, educational systems, political orders and daily lives provides handy justification for control, predictability and dominion and gives a largely false sense of security, satisfaction and fulfillment.[6] It asserts that things are important because they have a use-value for us. The 'rational' is the 'useful'. Things have no longer intrinsic intelligibility or 'rationality'; they have only use-value which we are free to use in any way we want.

Reason in the modern period has oscillated between the two extremes of logical positivism and radical historicism. The former view, represented by the Vienna Circle and its followers, has construed reason as an absolute and timeless principle unaffected by history, custom or such human frailties as emotion and desire. Rationality simply means proving that our concepts correspond to facts. It means drawing conclusions which fit the facts at hand. In this sense, rationality is essentially 'logical consistency' and finds its purest expression in formal logic and scientific method.[7] No other criteria count as a basis for rationality, and the value of everything from religion to art and education must be judged according to the logical and scientific dictates of this a-historic reason. Thus the values by which we are to live must be derived from the facts of nature which we must investigate through rational inquiry and logical analysis. All else is to be rejected as metaphysical nonsense. Reduced to a function of reasoning as formal logic, existence, too, is reduced to a logical term with no meaning and force outside logical-linguistic constructions.[8]

The second view, represented by the waves of postmodernism and constructivism since the 1960s, deconstructed reason to the point of turning it into a by-product of social historical processes. Like all other human traits and enterprises, reason is a historically constructed notion whose meaning and function varies from one social setting to another. Rationality means applying the human capacity for thinking to different problem-solving situations. It has meaning only in the context of specific issues, problems or research questions. Depending on the different types of human needs, rationality takes on new meanings and new functions. The defenders of this bounded view of reason insist that this is not to belittle the significance of reason or propose an irrational way of doing things. Rather, it is to admit the limitations of human reason. In this sense, rationality does not necessarily mean drawing conclusions that fit the facts. There are cases where the "anything goes" principle is more useful and functional than some abstract and mathematical notion of reason.[9]

The concept of reason has had a different trajectory in the Islamic tradition and avoided the extremes of positivist absolutism and radical relativism. The reason that emerged within the Islamic *Weltanschauung* proposed a different mode of thinking about existence, the universe, the human state and God. It was seen as part of a larger reality rather than a self-regulating principle and self-standing tool. It is this integrated and wholesale view of reality that underlies the Quranic mode of thinking about reason and rationality.

Ratio and Intellectus

Before moving further, a word of clarification is in order for the reason-intellect bifurcation that has come about as a result of a major philosophical transformation in the history of Western metaphysics. I shall not venture into this history as it requires a detailed treatment. It should be briefly pointed out, however, that *ratio* and *intellectus* came to designate two separate ways of looking at reality in the late Middle Ages and ever since then the two terms have taken different paths. *Ratio* has been used for logical analysis, abstraction, deduction, drawing conclusions, and other logical functions of reason. In this broad sense, *ratio* primarily constituted the basis of scientific knowledge and claimed precision and certainty. By contrast, *intellectus* came to designate intuitive and sapiential knowledge, which was now fully decoupled from rational investigation and logical analysis. By implication, it was seen as lacking a solid foundation like *ratio* because it spoke of such subjective terms as intuition, imagination, illumination but not proofs, evidence, and demonstration.

Had it not been for the later fallout between rationalist naturalism and mystical thought in the Western tradition, this may have been nothing more than a heuristic distinction. As a matter of fact, the thomistic tradition maintained a relationship of complementarity between *ratio* and *intellectus* and held that they were not opposed to one another but addressed to different aspects of the same reality[10] But as later history shows, the two terms were employed to represent two substantially different ways of understanding the world and making moral judgments. *Ratio* became the main instrument of natural sciences, which by now had divested nature of all of its intrinsic intelligibility and symbolic significance, and developed a separate modus operandi. The further estrangement of *ratio* from *intellectus* meant that 'rational analysis' was no longer to unveil the built-in intelligibility of things, their symbolic significance, or their spiritual value. Rationality created a new domain of truth for itself and bade farewell to our holistic experience of reality. Rationalism, coupled with naturalism and positivism, sought to reduce reality to the analytical competencies of the human mind and identified quantitative-calculative thinking as the only reliable way of knowing the reality of things. Even though contemporary Christian theologians have insisted that both *ratio* and *intellectus* together make up a proper process of knowing, the bifurcation of discursive and intuitive modes of thinking has played a key role in the secularisation of the modern world-picture and the profanization of nature. Such a distinction has never occurred in the Islamic tradition. The word *'aql* means both reason and intellect in the two senses discussed above. *'Aql* is innately capable of performing the two functions of logical analysis and intuitive knowing without a contradiction. Furthermore, it is the same *'aql* that guides our will in our moral choices. It is true that in the later Islamic intellectual tradition, the philosophers have introduced a general distinction between "rational investigation" (*bahth*) and "taste" (dhawq) i.e., realised knowledge. The two modes of thinking, however, complement each other and help us uncover the multi-layered structure of reality, which, after all, demands a multi-dimensional yet integrated approach. In the words of Mulla Sadra who epitomises this tradition, "True demonstration does not contradict witnessing based on unveiling (*al-shuhud al-kashfi*)".[11] When Muslims state, largely under the pressure of modern rationalism and out of inferiority complex against the West, that "Islam is the religion of reason/intellect", what they mean is not that the Islamic faith, or any faith for that matter, can be reduced to human reason. Such a claim would turn faith into an empirical statement or logical proposition. Faith, by definition, must have a dimension that goes beyond reason; otherwise there would be no need for divine revelation and the Prophets. What is beyond reason, however, does not mean anti-reason; it means supra-rational, that which transcends the cognitive competencies of the human reason. Supra-rational is not irrational because reason can admit what lies beyond its capacities. Such an admission is not illogical because it states not ignorance, agnosticism or blind faith but a self-reflective acknowledgment of limits. Reason cannot think without certain rules and principles. Freedom is not the abolishment of all limits and rules but the exercise of reason in conjunction with virtue.[12]

What is unique and even astounding about human reason is that it can set its own limits to what it can and cannot know. The self-delimitation of reason is a rational act and points to the larger context of existence and intelligibility within which it functions. This is what al-Ghazali attempted with his critique of Peripatetic philosophy whereby he critically tried to draw the limits of speculative reason in the field of pure metaphysics which he believed belonged to the "invisible world" (*'alam al-ghayb*). Committing himself to a similar task but working with different premises, Kant, too, sought to lay out the limits of reason in his *Critique of Pure Reason*: "Human reason has this peculiar fate that in one species of its knowledge it is burdened by questions which, as prescribed by the very nature of reason itself, it is not able to ignore, but which, as transcending all its powers, it is not able to answer".[13]

The Ontological Ground of Quranic Rationality

Long before the Greek philosophical texts were translated into Arabic, Muslims had an encounter with the concept of reason/intellect as outlined in the Quran and the Hadith. In sharp contrast to the period of the *Jahiliyyah*, "ignorance", Islam represented the era of faith, knowledge, reason, justice and freedom all at once. Entering Islam meant leaving the mental and social habits of the age of ignorance, polytheism, injustice and immorality. It meant establishing a new socio-political order based on reason, justice, equality and virtue. It also required a new ontology of reason to overcome polytheistic logic and moral cynicism. And this was possible only by introducing a new *Weltanschauung* and a new mode of thinking.

In order to understand the place of reason and rationality in the Quran and the later Islamic intellectual tradition, we thus need to explore the new ontological ground of reason and the mode of thinking which the Quran introduced and did so through stories, implorations, deductions, syllogisms, commands, warnings, praises, and promises of reward and punishment. The rich repertoire of logical deductions and moral exhortations which we find in the

Quran and the Hadith purport to awaken our conscience so that we can begin to use our sensate and rational faculties in a manner that befits our state of existence. The Quran says: *And indeed We have put forth for men in this Quran every kind of similitude in order that they may remember* (Al-Zumar, 39:27). The *mathal*, translated here as similitude, refers to metaphors and parables by which a fundamental message is conveyed – a message which may otherwise remain inaccessible to the human mind. But since no parable is devoid of cognitive content, this is an appeal both to reason and imagination so that we may "remember" what is essential.

The path of thinking which we find in the Quran is not comprised of assembling of facts; nor is it a pietistic enumeration of commands and prohibitions. Rather, it is a wholesome undertaking that requires setting upon an intellectual, moral and spiritual journey. It encompasses all of our being and overcomes such dualities as the sensate versus the rational, the material versus the spiritual, the individual versus the universe, nature versus culture, and so on. The integrated mode of thinking which the Quran embodies in its unique style reflects the nature of reality, which is interdependent and multilayered. It urges us to see the interconnectedness of things and how one thing leads to the other in the great chain of being.

The Quranic mode of thinking is then primarily not descriptive but prescriptive. The Quran does not simply describe things as facts or information; its suggestive stories, striking metaphors and vivid descriptions of God's creation and interventions in history are meant to change the way we see things and our place in the world. It seeks to transform the human conscience so that we can live a life based on justified faith and virtue.[14] Once this conscience is awoken and brought up to reckon with the reality of things, everything falls in place: our reason, thinking, sense organs, seeing, hearing, perceiving and moral judgments begin to come together. Reason and rationality arise within this larger context of integrated thinking and moral discernment. Far from being a principle and ground of truth by itself, reason functions within the larger context of our being in the world and the human responses we give to reality.

Owing its existence to something larger than what is purely human, reason cannot know God in the sense of 'encapsulating' Him because as a finite being, it cannot encircle that which is infinite. God cannot be known empirically because empirical knowledge entails limit, position, relation, relativity, etc., none of which applies to God. God can be known through reason/intelligence to the extent to which the Absolute and the Infinite can be intuited, grasped and represented through formal propositions, concepts, and metaphors. To expect reason to do more than that would be to transgress its own limits. If reason, like other components of reality, is part of the order of existence and not the whole of it, then it can never fully encapsulate the whole of reality. But this in no way diminishes or undermines its significance. By contrast, God is the absolute reality that encapsulates everything. He is *al-Muhit*, the One who encompasses everything. Thus the Quran says that *Vision perceives Him not, but He perceives [all] vision; and He is the Subtle, the Acquainted* (Al-An'am, 6:103).

Like love, charity, wisdom, spirituality and art, rationality is a fundamental human response to the call of reality. It enables us to disclose the intelligible structure of the order of existence. It invites us to overcome our corporeal existence and connect with the world of nature in primarily rational and moral terms. It urges us to establish a socio-political order based on virtue, justice and freedom. The Quran presents a view of the human person according to which our humanity is formed by 'rationality' (*'aql, nutq*) and those other traits that are equally central to our task to give a meaningful response to reality. In an ontological sense, this means recognising the reality of things as they are and see them as a "trust" (*amanah*) from God. The human response to the Divine call of protecting His trust is to become His "vicegerent" (*khalifah*) on earth and thus submit to God, which is the literal meaning of Islam. In the formal religious language, this submission is called *'ibadah*, worship, the supreme human act that transcends the limitations of human existence and binds us to the Absolute and the Infinite.

In this regard, the Quranic mode of thinking is not empirical or rationalist, historical or systematic, apodictic or pedagogical, analytical or descriptive. It is none of them and all of them at once. It combines conceptual analysis with moral judgment, empirical observation with spiritual guidance, historical narrative with eschatological expectation, and abstraction with imperative command. The Quran is primarily a "guidance" (*hidayah*) for mankind (Al-Baqarah, 2:2) and seeks to lead us from ignorance to knowledge, from darkness to light, from injustice and oppression to freedom. The Quranic rationality thus extends from the empirical and conceptual to the moral and the spiritual. Being rational means rejecting oppression and injustice and embracing the Divine call for justice. The Prophet of Islam has defined 'intelligent person' (*al-kayyis*) as one who "controls his ego and prepares for the afterlife" (Tirmidhi, 25). In Islamic law and theology, a person must be 'sane' or 'intelligent' (*aqil*) in order to be responsible for his/her actions because there is no religious responsibility (*taklif*) without having sanity or reason (*'aql*).

In the Islamic tradition, this forms the basis of the moral ontology of reason and rationality and establishes a strong connection between intelligence, rationality, faith and virtue. According to Harith al-Muhasibi (d. 857), reason is "a disposition that is known through its deeds".[15] It acts as a principle of moral action and seeks to bring us closer to the Divine. If a person is really intelligent, reasons al-Muhasibi, he will seek to secure his salvation in this world and in the hereafter, for which he must use his reason properly.

By basing his analysis on the "nobility of reason", which is the title of his work, al-Muhasibi wants to show the unique character of human reason for establishing a justified faith and a virtuous life. A proper use of reason, illuminated by faith, leads to rational thinking and moral behaviour. By the same token, faith articulated and corroborated by reason has depth and certainty. The 14th century philosopher Haydar Amuli sees perfect harmony between faith and reason and compares religion (*al-shar'*) and reason to the body and the spirit. Just as the spirit cannot function without the body, the body cannot find meaning, life and wholeness without the spirit. Thus "neither religion dispenses with reason nor reason with religion. Raghib al-Isfahani, quoted by Amuli, states in strikingly unambiguous terms that "reason can never find the right path without religion and religion can never have clarity without reason".[16] Logic and transcendence thus work together to reveal the nature of things and realise our humanity. But this can happen only when we see human reason working in a larger context of thinking and contemplation.

Reason and Thinking in Context

The verb 'a-q-l, to intellect or to use one's reason, literally means to hold, to protect and to guard. Reason is that by which we protect ourselves from falsehood, error and evildoing. Thus *ma'qal* means 'fortress'. This is the same meaning conveyed in the English phrase "intelligent person". This basic meaning of reason is not to be taken lightly, for it underlies the essential component of thinking and contemplation as the proper human response to the call of reality. In contrast to attempts to reduce reason and rationality to logical competency and procedural ratiocination, reason as a principle of truth and as an instrument of knowledge represents an encounter with the reality of things. Thinking is not simply to enumerate the physical properties of things or the logical relations of concepts. It is more than a mere mental representation of things because, as Muslim philosophers insist, mental abstraction gives us only a picture of reality. Like all mental abstractions, this picture is frozen and can never fully measure up to the reality itself.

Abstract concepts are essential for rational thinking and the formation of ideas. Thinking, however, requires more than abstraction and use of concepts. It takes place in a context of encounter with reality and puts us in a relationship with something larger than us. It means seeing, observing, listening, hearing, reflecting, contemplating, and drawing the appropriate practical and moral conclusions. It means responding to what we encounter. It involves rational analysis but also moral commitment. In its deepest sense, thinking prevents us from seeing things as a means to an end. It challenges instrumental rationality on both ontological and spiritual grounds. As I shall discuss shortly, if the world has been created by God, then it cannot be reduced to utility. It has a substantive meaning and value independent of us.

In principle, there is nothing essentially wrong with the idea that we attain a degree of rationality by following rules and procedures. Following a rule can certainly count as rational act and comes handy in our daily lives, scientific explorations, economic decisions, political lives, etc. But while it has its uses, instrumental rationality moves at the surface of human subjectivity and does not necessarily relate us to reality. Following a rule is no guarantee for a rational outcome. We may follow a procedure and arrive at certain conclusions. The outcome, though, can be the most irrational thing and even a catastrophe. Like many autocracies, the Nazis, for instance, had a rule-bound, procedurally 'rational' governance of Germany. But their instrumentalist approach to religion, history, science and politics destroyed the very meaning of being human. The content and substance of what we do must also have a rational basis.

The Quran subscribes to a substantive view of rationality by asserting that not only our instruments and procedures but also our fundamental notions and concepts should be properly rational and conform to the reality of things. The substantive view of rationality follows from the intrinsic intelligibility of existence as God's creation. Every rational act on our part is an act of conforming to the principle of reason built into the nature of things. Whatever violates this principle lands us in the realm of the irrational.

Substantive rationality is also supported by the anthropology of reason itself. Most Muslim thinkers hold that reason responds to empirical data and abstract notions through its own innate qualities. Far from being a hypothetical tabula rasa, reason reflects the fundamental traits of existence of which it is a part. Raghib al-Isfahani divides reason into two: *'aql matbu'*, "innate reason", and *'aql masmu'*, "acquired reason". *Masmu'* literally means that which is heard, referring to things learnt by hearing from others. It roughly corresponds to experience and refers to the context of human relations. Innate reason refers to our in-born ability to grasp the intelligible order and truth of things. It is through innate reason that we inhabit an intelligible world. Acquired reason is what we learn by 'hearing' from others and refers to the context of social relations and linguistic forms with which we name things.

The two are intertwined but 'innate reason' takes precedence over 'acquired reason'. Isfahani, who attributes this division to Imam Ali ibn Abi Talib, says that just as the light of the sun has no use when the eye is blinded, acquired reason can do no good when innate reason is corrupted.[17] Reason then works two-ways: in its innate form, it works from inside and out. It encounters and witnesses the visible world through its inborn qualities. This is part of *fitrah*, the fundamental human nature, which is our window to the world of existence and thus must be protected in order to 'see' right.[18] In its acquired form, reason moves from outside to inside and takes in bits and pieces of empirical data and impressions from the outside world. It is the combination of the two, the inner and the outer, that gives us a fuller picture of the function of reason vis-à-vis reality. This fundamental function of reason, however, always takes place within a larger context of ontological significance and epistemic competency.[19]

The most fundamental function of reason/intellect is to act as a mirror to reflect the intrinsic meaning and order of things. In performing this task, the intellect has a special relationship with the Divine because it emanates from the Divine Nature. What the intellect discovers as order, necessity and intelligibility in the universe is a reflection of God's own Nature and Will. Mulla Sadra provides a vivid description of this aspect of the intellect:

> The intellect, since there is no veil between it and the the First Truth [God], can witness by itself the essence of the Truth [God] … there is no veiling between the two … [God] can certainly manifest itself to the intellect and the manifestation here takes place through the lucid [unveiling] of [God's] essence. There is no aspect or quality added to the Divine and another being added to [the intellect]. The essence of the intellect is like a polished mirror on which the form of the Truth shines. On the mirror itself, there is no existential entity except the reflected form, and the reflected form is nothing but the form related to the Truth. Therefore in the essence of the intellect there is nothing other than the form of the Truth and *wa'l-ma'ad*. There are no two things here: the existence of the intellect and the manifestation of the Truth upon it because one being cannot have to existences. By the same token, two [distinct] forms cannot emanate from God in one single manner. Because of this, the sages (*'urafa'*) have said that God does not manifest [Himself] twice in the same form. Thus it is known that the existence of the intellect is nothing but a manifestation of God the Exalted through His Form on the intellect; and the form of God's essence is itself His own Essence, not something added to Him.[20]

The Vocabulary of Thinking in the Quran

The Quran uses a number of terms that are closely related to reason/intellect and thinking. *Tafakkur*, "thinking", *qalb*, "heart", *fu'ad*, "inner heart", and *lubb*, literally "seed" meaning "essential heart", are among these terms and each corresponds to a different aspect of the act of perceiving, thinking and reflecting. There are also other terms which fall within the same semantic field of *'aql*: *'ilm*, "knowledge"; *fahm*, "understanding"; *fiqh*, "perceiving/understanding"; *idrak*, "grasping"; *shu'ur*, "consciousness"; *burhan*, "demonstration"; *hujjah*, "evidence"; *bayyinah*, "clear evidence"; sultan, "overwhelming evidence", *furqan*, "discernment"; *tadabbur*, "contemplation"; *nutq*, "talking/thinking"; *hukm*, "judgment"; *hikmah*, "wisdom"; and *dhikr*, "remembrance/invocation". The Quranic usage of these terms, whose full exposition requires a separate study, establishes a context of integrated thinking in which our encounter with reality unveils different aspects of the all-inclusive reality of existence. More importantly, it leads to a mode of thinking that combines empirical observation, rational analysis, moral judgment and spiritual refinement.

This rich vocabulary points to the wholeness of perceiving and thinking. In contrast to categorical distinctions between sensate perception and conceptual analysis, our natural or 'first-order' encounter with things takes place as a unitary experience. In perceiving things, our sense organs and reason work together. The sharp distinctions between sensate qualities, which correspond to the physical-material world, and intellectual notions, which correspond to the world of the mind, are reflections of the Cartesian bifurcation between *res extensa* and *res cogitans* and hardly give us an accurate description of the actual act of perceiving and understanding. These categories belong to the 'second-order' reflection upon reality whereby we make distinctions between subject and object, the knower and the known, the perceiver and the perceived, mental and material, etc. Our first-order encounter with the world takes place in a different context.

The wholeness of our epistemic experience of things stems from the wholeness of existence. Knowing as encounter means that we stand before our object of knowledge. This puts us in a special relationship with the reality of things in that we respond to it through our epistemic faculties rather than create its meaning in a a self-referential way. This meaning of knowing through reason is reflected in one of the root meanings of the word *'aql*, which is to tie, to link, to relate. Reason ties us to the truth and thus opens up a new horizon beyond the ordinary chain of causes. In a horizontal way, the human reason moves between and across facts and concepts and links them to one another. In a vertical way, it links what is below to what is higher. The Quran insists on the convergence of the two axes of causality: horizontal, which regulates the world of physical causes, and vertical, which introduces the 'Divine command' (*amr*) into the natural realm. There is no contradiction between the two but they follow different rules. The day and night follow each other as part of the natural order in which we live and there is no breaking of this rule. But also *"when God wants something to happen,*

He says to it "be" and it is" (Yasin, 36:82). Each realm of existence requires a different type of thinking.

The elaborate vocabulary of sensing, reasoning and thinking which the Quran employs is necessitated by the nature of reality itself. A multi-layered and multi-dimensional reality cannot be perceived by a single cognitive method. It requires a larger tool-set of conceptual abilities. At this point, the Quran speaks of '*alam al-ghayb*, "the world of the invisible" and '*alam al-shahadah*, "the world of the visible". the invisible world refers to that realm of existence known to God alone. God has given intimations of this world but no comprehensive knowledge of it has been made available. While not accessible to the human experience, the invisible world guides our encounter with the world of visible existence and thus functions as a signpost for our conceptual analyses and moral judgments. In a metaphysical and moral sense, it regulates the affairs of the visible world in which we live. What is striking about the Quranic notion of the 'visible world' is that a proper perception of it is based on an experience of 'witnessing' (*mushahadah*), which is different from looking and seeing. Witnessing means standing before that which presents itself. It entails looking and seeing but also attending to. It is more like the experience of looking at a landscape and having a gestalt perception of it. In contemplating a landscape, we move between parts and whole and each time discover a new relationship.

In this sense, our encounter with the reality of things is a rational and conceptual process but takes place within a larger context of intelligibility and significance that goes beyond purely logical and discursive thinking. Concepts, which are not created in vacuum, correspond to different aspects of reality and emerge in our encounter with reality, which the Quran describes as "bearing witness to the truth". Thus we 'see' the light, 'touch' the wood, 'smell' the rose, 'taste' the cherry, 'perceive' the dimension, 'think of' the infinitude, 'have consciousness of' the nearness of the water, 'discern' between a thing and its shadow, 'understand' a command, 'respond' to a call, 'submit' to truth, 'accept' the evidence, 'contemplate' the meaning of life, and so on. Each of these epistemic acts says something about our mental and conceptual abilities with which we understand the world. But more importantly, they correspond to something outside us and expand the horizon of our subjectivity.

Reason, Heart and the Human Conscience

This is comparable to the unitary experience of reality like a moving landscape rather than a particular frame taken out of it for dissection. The Quran identifies the heart (*al-qalb*) as the proper locus of the unitary experience of reality. This is where perceptual experience, conceptual thinking and moral judgment blend together. Given the sentimentalization of the 'heart' since the Cartesian turn in Western philosophy, it should be noted that the Quran assigns a clearly epistemic and intellectual function to the heart. The verses that mention the heart refer to our deep conscience by which we see reality as a whole. It combines rational thinking and moral judgment. The heart, when clean and properly guided, presides over other epistemic faculties and enlightens them about the truth. Heart and reason function as a conduit for gaining insight into the reality of things and how we should relate ourselves to it. It is in this context that the Arabic linguists have identified *'aql* and *qalb* as being synonymous.[21] The goal of thinking through *'aql* and *qalb* is to disclose and inhabit the intelligible order from which particular beings in the universe derive their meaning. Muslim thinkers see no contradiction between reason and heart, rational thinking and contemplation, logic and transcendence. One of the major figures of the *Kalam* tradition, Abu Hayyan al-Tawhidi begins his famous work *al-Muqabasat* with a prayer to God to grant him "through His Grace and Generosity the spirit of the heart through the light of the intellect (*ruh al-qalb binur al-'aql*)".[22]

This is not surprising if we understand how our empirical and conceptual engagement with things works. Possessing sense organs is no guarantee for perceiving things properly because the senses are subsumed under a higher epistemic principle. After all, it is our reason that makes sense of what our sense organs perceive as a raw experience. We may have an eye with which to see but may see things in a distorted manner because of, say, a nervous breakdown.[23]

We may have two ears but may fail to hear because we may deliberately chose not to hear certain things. We may have a sharp mind but may not arrive at the right conclusion in, say, a legal dispute because our desire to win the case may take over our judgment. Our sensate faculties thus function within a larger context of conceptual, emotional and moral conditions. The process of arriving at the truth of something entails a unitary experience and involves sensate, cognitive, psychological and moral principles and considerations. al-Ghazali, following the tradition before him and basing his analysis on the hadith, describes sense organs as "the soldiers of the heart" and says that "the heart is like the king and the soldiers are like its servants and aids".[24] Even the physically sound functioning of the sense organs depends on the soundness and cleanliness of the heart.

The human person is endowed with reason and thus can have access to the reality of things. But his reason and judgment can be clouded by his ego and carnal desires. He may thus lose his ability for discernment and can delude himself into thinking that he knows and forgets the stubborn and commanding nature of the ego. Against this, the Quran warns:

> *Have you seen the one who takes as his god his own desire? Then would you be a guardian over him? {43} Or do you think that most of them hear or reason? They are only like cattle; nay, they are even farther astray from the Path. {44} (Al-Furqan, 25:43–44).*

Animals serve the purpose for which they have been created. But those who have been created to worship God take their own ego as their master and worship themselves even though they have been given clear signs. This is where their 'hearing' and 'reasoning' comes to no avail.[25] the Quran goes further and challenges those who claim to see and hear when in fact their conscience has been blinded:

> *And among them are those who listen to you. But can you cause the deaf to hear, although they will not use reason? {42} And among them are those who look at you. But can you guide the blind although they will not [attempt to] see? {43} Indeed, God does not wrong the people at all, but it is the people who are wronging themselves. {44} (Yunus, 10:42–44).*

> *And We have certainly created for Hell many of the jinn and mankind. They have hearts with which they do not understand, they have eyes with which they do not see, and they have ears with which they do not hear. Those are like livestock; rather, they are more astray. It is they who are the heedless. {179} (Al-A'raf, 7:179).*

This suggests that having sense organs is no guarantee to perceive the truth. Empirical knowledge by itself cannot reveal the truth of things. The heart and the sense organs, which are the "soldiers of the heart", must all be sound:

> *We made for them hearing and vision and hearts. But their hearing and vision and hearts availed them not from anything [of the punishment] when they were [continually] rejecting God's signs; and they were enveloped by what they used to ridicule." {26} (AlAhqaf, 46:26).*

The failure of seeing, hearing, etc., does not stem from a biological imperfection but from the closure of the mind and the heart to the truth. According to Ibn Kathir, this is a result of the fact that one does not "benefit from these organs which God has created as a cause for guidance".[26] In some respects, this is comparable to the vain effort to explain colours to the blind. The ontological disconnect that separates the visually blind from the experience of colours makes the discourse about colours impossible. But a greater illness is the illusion that we think we see things because we have eyes when in fact we do not see.[27] the Quran insists that 'seeing' as witnessing the truth requires a higher principle of intelligibility than bodily hearing and seeing:

> *Indeed, you will not make the dead hear, nor will you make the deaf hear the call when they have turned their backs retreating. {80} Nor can you lead the blind out of their error, you can only make to hear those who believe in Our proofs/signs, and those who have submitted [themselves to God]. {81} (Al-Naml, 27:80–81).*

Having sound sensate organs is then not enough; they need to be guided by intelligence and wisdom. As Plato says in Phaedrus 250, "sight is the most piercing of our bodily senses; though not by that is wisdom seen". The heart must be uncorrupted and untainted in order to function properly. Quoting the Quran and the Prophet of Islam, al-Tirmidhi (d. 910) concludes, in an important work on the heart attributed to him, that the "soundness of sensate organs is possible through the soundness of heart; their corruption comes with the corruption of the heart".[28] Thus *al-sadr* ("the chest"), *al-qalb* ("the heart), *al-fu'ad* ("the inner heart"), and al-lubb ("the innermost intellect"), which al-Tirmidhi analyses with great perspicacity, do not function as separate organs but rather provide a cognitive and spiritual context for our experience of the truth. A famous saying of the Prophet of Islam sums up this view of the heart and its relation to other faculties and sense organs: "Verily, there is in the body a small piece of flesh; if it is good, the whole body is good and if it is corrupted the whole body is corrupted. It is the heart." As the proper locus of *tasdiq*, 'confirmation' or 'corroboration', the heart gathers together sensate and conceptual knowledge and provides a unitary experience of reality. The Quran thus insists on the total soundness and integrity of our sensate, psychological and mental faculties in order for us to know, and advices us to "travel on earth". Travelling or journeying means to look at the entire landscape of existence and history in order to put things in perspective:

> *So have they not traveled through the earth and have hearts by which to reason and ears by which to hear? For indeed, it is not eyes that are blinded, but blinded are the hearts which are within the breasts." {46} (Al-Hajj, 22:46)*

Once the heart is blinded, all else is skewed and darkened. A similar danger is to act on *zann*, subjective opinion or conjecture, without sound evidence and firm foundation. Reason cannot accept conjecture as truth. Whether we conduct a scientific research or investigate the grounds of religious faith, we need more than conjecture on which to build our truth-claims. the same principle applies to human relations and moral attitude (see Al-Hujurat, 49:12). Truth, not conjecture must be the basis of justification for faith:

> *Say, "Are there of your 'partners' any who guides to the truth?" Say, "God guides to the truth. So is He who guides to the truth more worthy to be followed or he who guides not unless he is guided? Then what is [wrong] with you how do you judge? {35} And most of them follow nothing but conjecture. Certainly, conjecture can be of no avail against the truth. Surely, God is All-Aware of what they do." {36} (Yunus, 10:35–36; also Al-An'am, 6:116).*

As the presiding principle of sensate and cognitive faculties, the heart provides 'evidence' (*al-burhan*) and gives 'certainty' (*al-yaqin*). But this is contingent upon keeping the heart functioning properly in conjunction with reason and the soul to ensure certainty, integrity and tranquility "in the kingdom of the corporeal body of the human person" (*mamlakat al-badan al-insan*).[29] According to the spiritual anthropology of the Quran, one must constantly work on his heart, mind and conscience, and guard himself against falsehood. When a person persistently mistakes falsehood for truth and bases his judgment on pure conjecture and selfish desires, then he develops a certain habit of mind and loses his ability to distinguish between truth and error. When this happens, which is not rare given the enormous power of desires on reason, his heart becomes "sealed" and loses his conscience. Thus the phrase *God has sealed their hearts* should be understood not in a fatalistic manner whereby God has already ordained certain people to disbelief. this interpretation would go against the thrust of the Quranic message. Rather, when one keeps committing the same intellectual and moral mistake and does not repent, he develops a certain habit of misusing his reason, and God leaves those who deliberately persist on wrongdoing. A number of verses describe this closure of the heart/mind/conscience as a total loss of direction in both the intellectual and moral senses of the term:

> *Indeed, those who disbelieve it is all the same for them whether you warn them or do not warn them they will not believe. {6} God has set a seal upon their hearts and upon their hearing, and over their vision is a veil. And for them is a great punishment. {7} (Al-Baqarah, 2:6–7).*

> *And among them are those who listen to you, but We have placed over their hearts coverings, lest they understand it, and in their ears deafness. And if they should see every sign, they will not believe in it. Even when they come to you arguing with you, those who disbelieve say, "This is not but legends of the former peoples." {25} (Al-An'am, 6:25).*

> *The seven heavens and the earth and whatever is in them exalt Him. And there is not a thing except that it exalts [God] by His praise, but you do not understand their [way of] exalting. Indeed, He is ever Forbearing and Forgiving. {44} And when you recite the Quran, We put between you and those who believe not in the Hereather, an invisible veil. {45} And We have placed over their hearts coverings, lest they understand it, and in their ears deafness. And when you mention your Lord alone in the Quran, they turn back in aversion. {46} (Al-Isra', 17:44–46).*

When the hypocrites come to you, [O Muhammad], they say, "We testify that you are the Messenger of God." And God knows that you are His Messenger, and God testifies that the hypocrites are liars. {1} They have taken their oaths as a cover, so they averted [people] from the way of God. Indeed, it was evil that they were doing. {2} That is because they believed, and then they disbelieved; so their hearts were sealed over, and they do not understand. {3} (Al-Munafiqun, 63:1–3).

By contrast, those whose heart and conscience have been illuminated with the light of faith find peace and repose in the remembrance of God. This 'finding' is not something sentimental or imaginative; it touches the core of our existence and links us to God on the one hand, and to the reality of things on the other. It guides our thinking and acting in the world and saturates our lives with meaning. Thus the Quran says:

Those who believe and whose hearts find repose in the remembrance of God, verily, in the remembrance of God do hearts find rest. {28} (Al-Ra'd, 13:28).

It is He who sent down tranquility into the hearts of the believers that they would increase in faith along with their [present] faith. And to God belong the soldiers of the heavens and the earth, and ever is God Knowing and Wise. {4} (Al-Fath, 48:4).

In short, our conscience must be in the right place in order for our reason to function properly.

Reason, Existence and the Universe

The wholesale encounter with reality is a key component of the Quranic vocabulary of thinking and stems from the essential relationship between reason and existence. The word existence (*al-wujud*) is not used in the Quran. But the conceptual framework within which the world of creation is presented points to an order of existence in which God's creative act is disclosed. As the ground of all that exists, existence is a gift of Divine creation and derives its sustenance from God. In this sense, existence is the face of the Divine looking to the world of creation (*'alam al-khal*q). The created order displays various modalities of existence, which discloses and particularises itself into specific forms. While these forms or 'shares of existence' possess different qualities, they are united by the underlying reality of existence. The Quranic phrase *qul*, "everything" and "all", frequently used in the cosmological verses, refers to this aspect of existence: everything is interrelated to one another by virtue of the fact that they are created by the same God who, as we mentioned, is *Al-Muhit*, the 'one who encompasses everything'.

It is in this context that reason finds its proper relationship with existence. Existence is intrinsically intelligible because God creates optimally and what He creates has meaning, purpose and intelligibility built into it.[30] The following verse combines the purpose of creation, thinking and praying:

> *Do they not contemplate within themselves? God has not created the heavens and the earth and what is between them except in truth and for a specified term. And indeed, many of the people, in [the matter of] the meeting with their Lord, are disbelievers. {8} Have they not traveled through the earth and observed how was the end of those before them? They were greater than them in power, and they plowed the earth and built it up more than they have built it up, and their messengers came to them with clear evidences. And God would not ever have wronged them, but they were wronging themselves. {9} (Al-Rum, 30:8–9).*

God creates with wisdom (*hikmah*), purpose (*ghayah*) and providence (*'inayah*). As the ultimate source of all existence and intelligibility, God bestows these qualities on His creation and saturates the order of creation with meaning and purpose. The celebrated saying that "the first thing God has created is intellect *(al-'aql)*" should be understood in this context. The 'intellect' here refers to the universal principles of truth, order and intelligibility which God has built into the nature of things. The intellect is the first thing God has created because God creates things according to a certain order and principle. Thus "the intellect is the closest thing to the Divine".[31] In contrast to modern subjectivism, meaning is not simply a property of the mind. Just as knowledge cannot be reduced to the internal workings of the mind, as is the case with Descartes, meaning cannot be written off, a la Galileo, as a 'secondary quality' superimposed by the mind upon things either. Since meaning is not created but articulated and appropriated by the mind, its essence lies outside my mental constructions of it.

The moral import of this premise is clear: having a meaning and purpose in a non-subjective manner entails a tremendous sense of responsibility. Admitting that we, like the universe, have been created for a purpose means accepting a moral responsibility beyond ourselves. The Quran addresses the human person directly to make this point:

> *Do you then think that We have created you without a purpose and that you will not be returned to Us? The True Sovereign is too exalted above that. {115} (Al-Mu'minun, 23:115)*

> *Does man think that he will be leth wandering [at his own whim]? {36} (Al-Qiyamah, 75:36)*

As far as the universe is concerned, God creates things and the laws by which they exist. These laws, called *sunan Ilahiyya*, the universal laws of God, sustain the principles of order, harmony and continuity in the universe. It is the function of the human reason to discover these universal principles and intrinsic qualities. By applying itself to these principles, the intellect participates in the intelligible order of existence. Reason is able to discover these intrinsic modes of intelligibility because they are the intelligible principles built into the nature of reality. We can rationally and scientifically analyze the physical universe because it lends itself to such investigation in the first place. The Quran finds no contradiction between studying the universe as a natural phenomenon and seeing it as the supreme miracle of God.

The entire universe is an *ayah*, a "sign" for man from God

and points to something beyond itself. The Quran uses the same word, ayah, to refer to its verses as well as "God's signs" (*ayat Allah*) in the universe, which can be compared to what the Latins have called Vestigia Dei. The multiple meanings of ayah confirm the profound connections between God's verses in the scripture and His signs in the world of creation: both come from God; both are sacred; both are to be treated with utmost care; both require commitment. God's signs in the two senses are directly related to reason and rationality because they are addressed to the human reason so that man can understand the reality of things (theoretical reason) and pursue virtue and happiness (practical reason). Such a basic and 'material' fact as counting years and keeping time is indeed a "sign" for those who ponder over the order and regularity of the universe:

> *It is He who made the sun a shining light and the moon a light [for you] and determined for it phases that you may know the number of years and account [of time]. God has not created this except in truth. He details the signs (ayat) for a people who know. {5} Indeed, in the alternation of the night and the day and [in] what God has created in the heavens and the earth are signs for a people who fear God. {6} (Yunus, 10:5–6).*

God presents these signs to humans so that they can use their reason and derive the logical conclusion from them, which is to believe in God. Every sign in the Quran and the universe invites a response from the side of the human being. As Izutsu points out, humans can read these signs properly and "confirm" (*tasdiq*) their truth. Or, they fail to use their reason, succumb to their desires and thus "reject" (*takdhib*) their truth. While the first response leads to sincere faith with certainty, the second lands us in disbelief (*kufr*) and denial.[32] Misreading God's "clear signs" disconnects us from the reality, and can imperil salvation: And they will say: '*Had we but listened or used our intelligence, we would not have been among the dwellers of the blazing Fire!*' (Al-Mulk, 67:10). Only those who can really use their reason can understand the true meaning of "signs" and act accordingly: *We have made clear to you the signs if you shall use your reason, the Quran says* (Al `Imran, 3:118).

Those who use their reason can begin to decipher the non-linguistic language of the universe and understand how it submits to God. This deeper wisdom helps us see the difference between the one who is blind and the one who sees. The Quran is forceful in asserting that denying God and taking partners unto Him goes against the nature of things and violates the principle of reason:

> *And unto God Alone falls in prostration whoever is in the heavens and the earth, willingly or unwillingly, and so do their shadows in the mornings and in the athernoons. {15} Say: "Who is the Lord of the heavens and the earth?" Say: "(It is) God." Say: "Have you then taken (for worship) protectors other than Him, such as have no power either for benefit or for harm to themselves?" Say: "Is the blind equal to the one who sees? Or darkness equal to light? Or do they assign to God partners who created the like of His creation, so that the creation (which they made and His creation) seemed alike to them." Say: "God is the Creator of all things, He is the One, the Irresistible". {16} (Al-Ra'd, 13:15–16)*

Once this is clarified, observation, logical analysis, contemplation and praying join together:

> *And to God belongs the dominion of the heavens and the*

> *earth, and God is over all things competent. {189} Indeed, in the creation of the heavens and the earth and the alternation of the night and the day are signs for those of understanding. {190} Who remember God while standing or sitting or [lying] on their sides and give thought to the creation of the heavens and the earth, [saying], "Our Lord, You did not create this in vain; exalted are You [above such a thing]; then protect us from the punishment of the Fire. {191} Our Lord, indeed whoever You admit to the Fire – You have disgraced him, and for the wrongdoers there are no helpers. {192} Our Lord, indeed we have heard a caller calling to faith, [saying], 'Believe in your Lord,' and we have believed. Our Lord, so forgive us our sins and remove from us our misdeeds and cause us to die with the righteous. {193} Our Lord, and grant us what You promised us through Your messengers and do not disgrace us on the Day of Resurrection. Indeed, You do not fail in [Your] promise." {194} (Al `Imran, 3:189–194).*

According to the Quran, the creation of the universe by God is so reasonable and self-evident that reason, unhindered by irrational causes, immediately recognises it. This grasping of the truth through intuition (*hads*) underlies much of our empirical and conceptual knowledge. Those who recognise the truth when they see it do in fact use their reason in the most proper way. The Quran uses the phrase *ulu'l-albab*, "those who have deep understanding of things" to distinguish them from those who are merely interested in being smart. *Al-Bab*, plural of *lubb*, meaning the essence and core of something, refers to a deeper perception of the reality of things which we understand through our reason. According to Ibn Kathir, *ulu'l-albab* refers to those "complete and perspicacious intellects which perceive the reality of things in their apparent reality".[33] Qurtubi describes them as those who "use their reason in contemplating proofs".[34] Once reason is put to proper use, it obtains new degrees of understanding, and the categorical distinctions between reasoning, contemplating and praying evaporate. This is when one begins to obtain certainty (*al-yaqin*), which leaves no doubt about the truth of something standing before us. At this point, the Quran puts so much emphasis on the selfevident and clear nature of the truth that it forbids forcing people into converting to Islam. Instead, they should be able to see the truth by themselves:

> *There is no compulsion in religion. Verily, the Right Path has become distinct from the wrong path. Whoever disbelieves in Taghut and believes in God, then he has grasped the most trustworthy handhold that will never break. And God is All-Hearer, All-Knower. {256} (Al-Baqarah, 2:256).*

The 'language of the universe' is revealed to human reason in the form of strict orders, laws, principles, patterns but also powerful symbols, parables and metaphors. The Quran sees no contradiction between strict rules of logic, which come from nothing but God's own Nature, and the symbolism of creation. the Quran invites us to discover the perfect order God has created in the universe. The order and regularity that come with this is a proof for the existence of an intelligent Creator. But we are also expected to grasp the symbolic language of the universe and how it praises God at every moment.

> *The seven heavens and the earth and whatever is in them exalt Him. And there is not a thing except that it exalts Him by His praise, but you do not understand (tafqahuna) their [way of] exalting. Indeed, He is ever Forbearing and For-*

giving. {44} (Al-Isra', 17:44).[35]

A reductionist and rationalist approach, which dwarfs our cognitive capacities and atrophies our imaginative powers, prevents us from understanding the non-discursive language of the universe. The world of creation has a constant conversation with its Creator because it is a 'Muslim' (Al `Imran 3:83), i.e., that which surrenders to God. The humans share this quality with nature with one fundamental difference: they have free will (*iradah*) and must chose faith over disbelief, truth over falsehood, and virtue over vice.[36]

A person who has perfected his sense of discernment can intuit and grasp the universe praising God. This intuitive and 'imaginative' thinking is not outside the ken of reason because reason, as I have been arguing, can accommodate non-formal articulations of the truth and understand the non-discursive insights we gain in our encounter with reality.

Rationality and Morality

The same intuitive thinking is at work in our moral choices. Since moral principles are self-evident in most cases, we know how we need to act in such situations. But is it enough to have a self-evident argument to be able to act virtuously? Given the driving force of human emotions, even the correct use of reason alone cannot be sufficient to always make the right moral choices. The reason is that we have to combine reason and will, the two distinguishing features of being human, in order to act on what we believe. In contrast to Descartes who called the human person a "machine who thinks", we are also beings who bear will. Here 'will' does not simply designate choosing one option or the other. It refers to our ability to make a choice from among available possibilities. But in an axiological sense, it means choosing truth over falsehood and good over evil. Reason and rationality in the broad sense discussed above guide our choices and form the content of our moral behaviour. Rationality and morality thus go hand in hand because we are rational animals and moral beings at the same time.

In the Quran, this point is registered in the relationship between using reason and having a moral and spiritual awareness of God. The word *taqwa*, usually translated as consciousness and fear of God, literally means to protect and guard oneself against danger. In the tradition, it refers to "protecting the soul from what afflicts it".[37] As explained in the Hadith, *taqwa* means having the majestic presence of God in one's heart by which to protect oneself against everything false, evil and ugly. In this sense, the conceptual meanings of '*aql* and *taqwa* converge: they both refer to our conscious effort to protect ourselves against the inhuman and immoral consequences of evildoing, injustice and oppression. Thus "the intelligent person is the one who has consciousness (*taqwa*) of his Lord and who reckons with his soul".[38]

This principle underlies the rational basis of choosing goodness over evil and virtue over vice. Reason has no problem with accepting 'consciousness of God' (*taqwa*) as a moral and spiritual principle because it guides our moral choices. It is only by combining intelligibility, meaning and will that we fulfill our humanity as 'rational animals'. Moral choices make sense not because simply they are our free choices but because they let us participate in the intelligible order of existence and thus enable us to go beyond ourselves and reach out to a larger reality. According to the Islamic ethical tradition, upholding justice makes sense because justice ('*adl*) means "putting things in their proper place". Likewise, opposing injustice is reasonable because injustice (*zulm*) means "putting things out of their place", i.e., destroying the order which gives meaning to things. An act is rational when it conforms to the reality of something and pays due attention to its proper place. It then makes perfect sense to protect oneself against the destructive forces of selfishness and evil-doing; acting otherwise contradicts the basis of our humanity. Summing up these points, Ibn Miskawayh says: "...since justice consists indeed giving to the right person what ought to be given in the right way, it would be inconceivable that men should not owe God, exalted is He, who granted us all these immense goods, an obligation which they should fulfill".[39]

We can then conclude that it is rational to be moral. By the same token, immorality is irrational because it goes against our self-interest and violates the order of things, which, in turn, causes us harm. The Quranic treatment of moral choices and how they are made within the larger context of existence establishes rationality as a key component of moral behaviour. But the reverse is also true: rationality, carried to its full capacity, results in moral behaviour and extends to other human beings, the universe and eventually God. According to the Quran, human beings have been granted reason to discern between right and wrong on the one hand, and good and evil on the other. In terms of both true knowledge and moral behaviour, we use reason to make the right choices. The famous controversy among Muslim theologians over whether we know things to be true and good because they are intrinsically so or because God has created them in that way is irrelevant here. The key point is that correct thinking and moral behaviour complement each other and thus reject any dichotomy between reason, rationality, belief and morality. Thus Ibn Hazm says that "knowledge has a decisive role in the implementation of virtues … knowledge has a share in each and every virtue and ignorance in each and every vice".[40] In a similar vein, Ibn Miskawayh identifies "the intelligent man" as one who seeks "virtue in his rational soul, examine the imperfections of this soul in particular, and strives to remedy them to the extent of his capacity and effort".[41]

Rationality as Coherence

The move from reason and rationality to moral behaviour and back is a recurrent theme in the Quran and forms the basis of the Islamic ethical tradition. Reason, when properly cultivated, leads to moral action; moral behaviour, in turn, nurtures reason. The Quran considers this simple syllogism to be self-evident because it is a contradiction to accept something as right and true and then not act accordingly. So is hypocrisy: *Do you order other people to be righteous and forget yourselves while you recite the Scripture? Will you, then, not reason?* (Al-Baqarah, 2:44). the Quran condemns hypocrisy as much as disbelief and in some cases more so because hypocrisy, besides being a failure of the human will, breaks the logical connection between reason and morality and thus lands us in incoherence. *O you who have believe, why do you say what you do not do? {2} It is most hateful in the sight of God that you say that which you do not do."* {3}(Al-Saf, 61:2-3).

The same principle of coherence applies to belief in God. The cosmological verses in the Quran, which give vivid descriptions of how God has created the universe and the human being, make a strong case for rationality as coherence because all of them without exception speak to the human reason to make the logical connection between a universe so miraculously ordered and well-functioning and the belief in the Creator who created it. Those who take partners unto God, while believing in His existence, contradict themselves. Believing in God and not heeding His guidance presents a clear case of incoherence.

The following verses, while emphasising God's infinite mercy in creating and caring for the humankind, challenge the internal inconsistency of taking partners unto God (shirk), which is the greatest sin, and declares it to be utterly irrational. Those who think, ponder and use their reason have no difficulty in recognising God as He deserves to be recognised.

> *And who other than Him created the heavens and the earth and sent down for you water from the sky, whereby We cause to grow lush orchards; for it is not up to you to cause their trees to grow! Is there, then, a god besides God? Yet these are the people who ascribe partners to Him. {60} And who other than Him made the earth a firm abode [for you], and set rivers traversing through it, and put firm mountains therein and sealed off one sea from the other? Is there, then, a god besides God? Indeed, most of them do not know. {61} And who other than Him responds to the distressed one when he calls Him and He relieves him of the distress and Who has made you [mankind] His vicegerents on earth? Is there, then, a god besides God? – little do you reflect! {62} And Who other than Him guides you in the darkness of the land and the sea? And who sends forth winds heralding His mercy? Is there, then, a god besides God? Far exalted be He above what they associate with Him! {63} And who other than Him brings forth His creation and then re-creates it? And who gives you sustenance from the heaven and*

> *the earth? Is there, then, a god besides God? Say [O Muhammad!]: Bring your proof if you are right [in associating others with God]. {64} (Al-Naml, 27:60-64)*

These verses reveal a strongly argumentative approach and underlie the Quran's insistence on coherence as a basis for a proper discourse about the relationship between man and God on the one hand, God and the universe on the other. Rationality as coherence means that we draw the correct conclusions from the correct premises. Considering the continuity of our ontological and moral presuppositions, this suggests that our empirical observations about the universe lead to their logical conclusion in a theistic context, i.e., accepting God as God and acting accordingly. The Quran makes profuse use of this procedural notion of rationality and applies it to cosmological, theological and legal issues.

In its numerous confrontations with the Meccan pagans, the Quran challenges them to think for themselves and see if their misguided thinking about God makes any sense. A rationally coherent notion of God and the universe can be obtained through correct thinking if we can use our reason cogently to read the signs in the "visible world".

Islam and Science: Notes on an Ongoing Debate

In his preface to Heisenberg's *Physics and Philosophy*, F. S. C. Northrop made the following observation on the spread of modern science to non-Western societies:

> "...modern ways are going to alter and in part destroy traditional customs and values. It is frequently assumed by native leaders of non-Western societies, and also often by their Western advisers, that the problem of introducing modern scientific instruments and ways into Asia, the Middle East and Africa is merely that of giving the native people their political independence and then providing them with the funds and the practical instruments ... one cannot bring in the instruments of modern physics without sooner or later introducing its philosophical mentality, and this mentality, as it captures the scientifically trained youth, upsets the old familial and tribal moral loyalties."[42]

Northrop, who made these remarks more than four decades

ago, did not have to wait too long to see his predictions come true. The changes brought about by modern science in the minds and lives of people in the non-Western world have been no less profound than they are for people living in the Western hemisphere. The crisis of legitimacy and the dissolution of traditional certainties, closely related to the scientistic worldview of modern natural sciences, have a deep impact on how people in the Islamic world relate to the question of science on the one hand, and their intellectual and scientific tradition, on the other. From Muslim scientists and professionals who take science to be a pure and disengaged study of natural phenomena with no hidden ideological assumptions to those who consider modern science essentially physicalist, reductionist and in conflict with the ethos of the religious view of the universe, there is a wide range of views on where exactly science stands in the overall order of things. Regardless of what particular position one takes, the urgency of addressing the question of (modern) science is as fresh and challenging today as it was more than a century ago for Jamal al-Din Afghani, the father of Islamic modernism in the 19th century, and his generation.

There are two important components to the debate. The first pertains to the practical needs and concerns of Muslim countries. Keeping up with modern science and technology is the number one priority of governments in the Muslim world, as it is in fact everywhere else, and every year billions of dollars are allocated for science education, research, and transfer of technology. From Mustafa Kemal Ataturk, the founder of modern Turkey, to Mahathir Muhammad, the Prime Minister of Malaysia, the goal has remained the same: to fill the gap between Western and Islamic societies by empowering Muslim countries with the blessings of modern science. Not only the ruling elites but also the populace at large are convinced of the intrinsic power and necessity of science and technology, for this is where the superiority lies in the West. Contrary to the claims of "Oriental sleep", Muslim countries are no less pragmatic and utilitarian in their quest for power-through-technology than their European and American counterparts.

The second component concerns the intellectual domain and links the discussion both to modern science and its philosophical foundations and the Islamic scientific tradition as an alternative way of studying the order of nature. The philosophical foundations and, by derivation, built-in presuppositions of modern science and its historical rise in Europe have long been debated and well analysed. Long before the Kuhnian and post-modernist criticisms of modern science as a cultural product embedded in socio-historical necessities, a number of important studies sought to show how philosophical, cosmological, religious and metaphysical ideas played instrumental roles in the shaping of the modern scientific worldview from Galileo to Newton. Edwin Burtt's *The Metaphysical Foundations of Modern Physical Sciences* and Frances A. Yates' *Giardano Bruno and The Hermetic Tradition, inter alia*, were major challenges to the 19th century view of science as studying natural phenomena from a standpoint which Thomas Nagel has aptly described as 'view from nowhere', viz., seeing the world not from a particular point in it but rather over it, hence assuming an a-historical position. In what follows, I shall focus on how the Muslim world has responded to this debate and what possible positions we may expect to arise from these responses.

Scientific Universalism versus Cultural Particularism

The participation of Muslim philosophers and scholars in the debate over the historicity of modern science has added a new dimension to the debate in that the defenders of a scientific tradition rooted in Islamic metaphysics and cosmology have clearly argued for the cultural specificity and differentiation of scientific traditions. Such advocates of Islamic science as Seyyed Hossein Nasr, Naquib al-Attas, Osman Bakar, Muzaffar Iqbal, to name but a few, have defended a kind of cultural particularism against scientific universalism whereby the a-historical claims of modern scientism (and not science as such) to universal truth and validity are rejected and alternative ways of studying the order of nature are maintained. This is best illustrated in the sharp contrast between the religious-sacred view of nature and the secular outlook of modern science. While the great religious traditions have developed a complex cosmology and approached the world of nature as imbued with intrinsic intelligibility and order, modern scientism regards metaphysical and aesthetic considerations about the world of nature as philosophically unfounded and scientifically inconsequential.

Bertrand Russell's celebrated essay called "A Free Man's Worship", for instance, was written as a testimonial to this view of science. If we accept, according to Russell, the scientific view of the universe as *a theory of everything*, we will be saved from the 'confusions' of both philosophy and religion at once.

> "Such in outline, but even more purposeless, more void of meaning, is the world which Science presents for our belief. Amid such a world, if anywhere, our ideals henceforward must find a home. That Man is the product of causes which had no prevision of the end they were achieving; that his origin, his growth, his hopes and fears, his loves and his beliefs, are but the outcome of accidental collocations of atoms; that no fire, no heroism, no intensity of thought and feeling, can preserve an individual life beyond the grave; that all the labors of the ages, all the devotion, all the inspiration, all the noonday brightness of human genius, are destined to extinction in the vast

> death of the solar system, and that the whole temple of Man's achievement must inevitably be buried beneath the debris of a universe in ruins -all these things, if not quite beyond dispute, are yet so nearly certain, that no philosophy which rejects them can hope to stand".[43]

Russell's radical scientism has lost much of its élan today. But it remains the unwritten code of the popular perceptions of science. Furthermore, the stark contrast that we see between Russell's view of science and traditional cosmologies is also to be found within the Western intellectual tradition and especially in regards to such controversies as evolution versus creationism. The contrast is sharper in the case of Islamic thought and the reason lies in the different ways the Western and Islamic worlds have experienced secular modernity: while the secularisation of the Western view of nature was part and parcel of early and middle modernity, the Muslim world has largely avoided radical secularisation until recently. Even today, secularisation remains a top-down movement in most Muslim countries, imposed through Western education and state apparatus.

It is obvious that construing modern science as a particular and not the only way of studying natural phenomena poses a serious challenge to the exclusivist and absolutist claims of modern natural sciences that reduce reality to what can be measured empirically. To better understand this point about modern Western science, we may remember the distinction between the context of discovery and the context of justification. While the context of discovery refers to what the scientist actually does in her lab, the context of justification refers to how the scientist's work is interpreted and articulated in different frameworks of analysis. Insofar as the context of discovery is concerned, we may be justified in assuming a linear historical line that connects Ptolemy, Abu Bakr al-Razi or Nasir al-Din al-Tusi to Newton or Max Planck: the successes or failures of these scientists of different historical periods and cultural settings can be explained in terms of the accumulation of scientific knowledge, refinement of measurement, exactitude in prediction, advancement in taxonomy, etc. What they all have in common is the continuity of the context of discovery whereby religious and cultural elements, the "soft realities" of science, have a relatively small role to play.

The issue takes on a substantially different form when we move to the next level, i.e., the context of justification in which we attempt to understand and interpret the *meaning* of the empirical work of the scientist on the ground. Here, we are no longer in the world of the 'bare facts' of science, a set of primary qualities which constitute the physical reality of substances without any suppositions and interpretive domains. As much as the scientist would like to envision a "pure science" untainted by socio-cultural, historical, mythological or religious ideas, the very concept of 'bare facts' as the building blocks of scientific procedures is highly questionable. Science is not a mirror juxtaposed against the world and the scientist the incorrigible interpreter of the reality of things. Rather, every interpretation, extrapolation, deduction, induction, and even prediction is screened through a set of philosophical assumptions whether they are articulated explicitly or remain tacit. It is at this level of analysis that science becomes a cultural artifact bound by particular traditions, postulations, and needs. The basic tenets of modern science, which make it a secular enterprise, are all produced at the context of justification and can be accepted, questioned and/or rejected primarily on philosophical grounds.

The multiplicity of scientific worldviews is part and parcel of every scientific tradition in that the findings of a particular scientist or in a particular field of science are interpreted in a variety of ways that may or may not agree with other interpretations. In fact, this was the case in traditional societies where we always have multiple cosmologies both across and within specific traditions. Take the case of Islamic and Christian cosmologies. Both traditions produced elaborate cosmological schemes tightly linked to the astronomy and physics of their times, i.e., the Ptolemaic-Aristotelian astronomy. Naturally, the cosmology of Dante's *Divine Comedy* was structured along the lines of Biblical and Christian thought whereas Islamic cosmology was the result of a deliberate attempt to reconcile Greek-Aristotelian cosmology with Quranic theology and eschatology. Yet, we still find more cases of plurality within each of these traditions. The scholastic-Thomistic view of nature is not the same as St. Francis of Asisi's mystical and poetical deliberations of nature. In the same way, certain parts of Ibn Sina's Neoplatonic cosmology or that of the Brethren of Purity are considerably different from Ibn al-'Arabi's "Five Divine Presences" and Mulla Sadra's *mundus imaginalis.*

The case for particularism and the multiplicity of interpretations within and across cultural traditions does not lead to parochialism. It is possible to draw multiple conclusions from the same data both in science and philosophy, and as such plurality does not invalidate the veracity and relevance of divergent readings. The apparent diversity of traditional cosmologies is rooted in an underlying unity in that such postulates as the universe as a sign of God (*ayat Allah* in Arabic and *vestigia Dei* in Latin), teleology, intrinsic intelligibility of the world, order and harmony are all shared by various schools of thought. Tradition is not monolithic, and the same applies to the science(s) practiced within its bosom.

At this point, the concept of Islamic science has a lot to offer to the current religion-science debate. But this is true only if the term is understood in a broader sense to include the reassertion of the religious view of the universe as an alternative vision to the profane and secular worldview of modern scientism. Considering the eroding impact of scientism on traditional beliefs and practices and the disastrous consequences of scientific and technological development without boundaries, the Islamic world can make a strong case for a new vision of science that will both cater to the vital needs of modern society and preserve the spiritual and ethical significance of the world of nature – a case for which people of other religious traditions have to collaborate to foster a common ground for a science that is in peace and harmony with both heaven and earth at the same time.

The Islamic World and Science Today

The Islamic intellectual and scientific tradition, going back to the rise of Islam as a world civilisation in the 9th and 10th centuries, remains a major source of pride and inspiration for the contemporary Muslim world in its quest for self-identity and self-esteem. The glory of Islamic civilisation stretching from Andalusia and the Balkans to Persia and India and the historic contributions of such Muslim scientists as Ibn al-Haytham, Jabir ibn Hayyan, Khwarazmi, Ibn Sina, al-Majriti, Nasir al-Din al-Tusi and others to the development of science are remembered throughout the Islamic world as more than a mere grandeur of the past. Rather, this tradition of remarkable scientific achievement and philosophical articulation is a witness to the study of the world of nature within a religious and sacred framework that delivered to both the spiritual and practical needs of human society.

The big challenge is to show the relevance of this tradition today without slipping into romanticism and without succumbing to the temptations of secular scientism. There is a world of difference between Ibn Sina's Neoplatonic cosmology and modern science not only in terms of cumulative knowledge and heuristic advancement but also in the philosophical outlook of the two systems of the universe. For a devout follower of modern science like John Searle, "there is really nothing in the universe but physical particles and fields of force acting on physical particles"[44], and this makes matters supposedly easier once we rest our case for a spiritual vision of the universe. The question for the Islamic world, however, is this: after four centuries of not practicing science in full scale and for the last century and a half trying to transfer science and technology from the West, will the Islamic world ever be in a position where it will put its own 'paradigm' in place and re-develop a scientific tradition that will be in harmony with its religious tenets and aspirations on the one hand, and cater to its practical needs, on the other?

The confusion that plagues the minds of countless scientists in the Muslim world and across the globe arises from the lack of a balance between the discourse and practice of science in an Islamic context. For some, the question of religion or any other philosophical consideration is simply not there. The scientist goes about her own work and fulfills her function in her scientific community without bothering herself with any 'big questions'. In most cases, however, the Muslim scientist is split between her profession as a scientist and her value system as a believer. The scientist works as part of a global scientific community and remains mostly indifferent to questions of ethics, cosmology, religion, etc. The believer practices her religion but brings very little from her devotion to bear on his scientific work. We thus end up with split identities and with very little ground to integrate the two in an intelligible and cogent manner.[45]

Part of the problem has to do with the resistance of the scientisticly minded Muslim professionals to accept any alternative to modern science except, perhaps, when it comes to the ethical and environmental misdeeds of modern science. This is a common phenomenon in spite of the fact that the groundwork for an Islamic concept of science and its conceptual scheme has already been done by a long list of Muslim scholars that include S. H. Nasr, Rene Guenon, O. Bakar, Alparslan Acikgenc, Muzaffar Iqbal, Mahdi Golshani, Ziauddin Sardar, Zaki Kirmani, and others with important differences among them.[46] The task at hand, however, is rendered more difficult by the simple nonexistence of a strong scientific tradition in the Muslim world. The possibility of applying an Islamic framework of science to actual scientific work is alarmingly limited in the sense that the level of scientific infrastructure in Muslim countries from physics and engineering to medicine and astronomy is simply not comparable with that of the West which controls the pace and direction of scientific research and technological innovation. Furthermore, the global network of scientific programs and technological novelties, funded by governments and powerful transnational corporations, makes it near impossible for any scientist to go against the grain and open up new venues for an alternative vision of the universe.

Until the Islamic world recovers its intellectual and scientific tradition on the one hand, and comes to terms with the challenges of modern science, on the other, we will either join the camp of scientific universalism and reduce reality to what the natural sciences can measure, or join the camp of radical anti-realism of the postmodernists, as it has othen been the case among the Muslim critics of secular science, and deny any validity to science. The Islamic intellectual and scientific tradition can provide a comprehensive framework which will address the challenge of studying the universe in a non-reductionist way and preserve the sacred meaning of nature – a framework shared by other religious traditions from Judaism and Christianity to traditional Hinduism and Buddhism.

Knowing the Self and the Non-Self

Towards a Philosophy of Non-Subjectivism

The celebrated Delphic dictum "Know thyself"[47] has been the subject of numerous commentaries for over two millennia. Greeks, Romans, Jews, Christians, Muslims, religious and secular philosophers have approached the subject from a variety of angles, offering many insights into the depths of the human soul, knowledge and what it means to be human. While most of these commentaries focus on the self for both pedagogical and philosophical reasons, they also say something about self-knowledge as a key component of spiritual life.

I shall concentrate on the two words "know" and "thyself" from a philosophical point of view and explore the underlying relationship between the self, knowledge, and the non-self. In knowing ourselves, we also know the non-self, i.e., that which is outside the self and that this binary relationship between the self and the non-self takes us beyond the dichotomies of the modern self against the world and against others. Self-knowledge has deep moral and spiritual consequences.

Modes of Knowing

Let's start with our claim to know. To know means several things. For the sake of expediency, I shall limit them to three. The first is to produce a mental image of things outside the mind. This we do by grasping the intelligible forms of things. As Aristotle and later al-Farabi said, we can only know the intelligible forms of things, not their matter. My knowledge of the chair in front of me is based on my perception of the form of the chair, not its matter even though it might be through sensation, i.e., seeing and touching the chair. Here, what counts as knowledge is a mental image. Ibn Sina calls this representational knowledge *(al-'ilm al-irtisami)* whereby the form of what I know is imprinted on my mind. The distinction between subject and object is clearly stated, and knowledge is defined as the extrapolation and formulation of the latter in terms of the former.

The second kind of knowledge is to establish logical relations between concepts. I relate the color red to the color blue and say that they are different from one another. Or, I relate the term "humanity" to Socrates and say that Socrates is human. Still, I attribute the term impossible to things or cases which we consider to be impossible. In all of these, I work across and between concepts without concerning myself with the intelligible forms of things in the outside world. This is how we move from one concept to another, from the better known to the lesser known. This is also how we regulate our thoughts through such terms as cogency, consistency, possibility, correlation, contrast, and so on.

The two forms of knowledge above form the basis of our knowledge in its various modes. In both cases, we operate within a framework of subject–object duality and regulate our thoughts accordingly. But there is a third kind of knowledge, which underlies both forms of knowledge mentioned above. Put simply, it is knowledge as encountering existence or more properly an aspect of it. I say an aspect of it because we perceive existence not existence-qua-existence but through one of its modalities.

If existence is the ground of all there is, then all knowledge is an encounter with existence. What we know and conceptualise as knowledge is ultimately nothing but an aspect of existence. We may well remember Husserl's phenomenological insight that knowledge is always the *knowledge of* something. In a phenomenological sense, consciousness is always the consciousness of "something" and entails an "openness, directedness to the other, and denial of self-foundation. In this way consciousness appears to be not pure interiority, but should be understood as a goingout-of-itself, as ek-sistence."[48] We have to think about knowledge not just in terms of concepts, notions but also in terms of what counts as the ground of knowledge. Now, this something of which Husserl speaks cannot be other than existence.

Existence and Cognition

So, every claim to knowledge, whether sensate or conceptual, is a claim to encounter and eventually unveil an aspect of existence. In knowing things and ourselves, we participate in the reality of existence which reveals itself in countless modes, colours and shapes. Here knowledge is no longer simply my mental construction of things or establishing relations between abstract notions. If understood in the ontological sense of the term, to know is to participate in the intelligible reality of existence and go beyond the limits of my mind's internal procedures.

The key point here is the fact that existence precedes cognition. We *are* before we know. Something *is* before it is known. In other words, something must first exist before we can know it. Mulla Sadra, one of the brilliant heirs of Ibn al-'Arabi's philosophy of existence, would go so far as to equate knowledge with existence and say that "knowledge is a modality of existence". In this sense, our epistemic claim to know things is secondary to their ontological reality. It is true that since it is we who claim to know existence or anything else, we have to know something about the way we know. As suggested by the course of modern philosophy since Descartes, we should perhaps start with the human mind and work our way to existence and other things outside the mind. But this is to put the cart before the horse. Making knowledge or the human mind the beginning of our philosophical inquiry is to produce a concept of existence in terms of how the mind knows it rather than how it fits into the all-inclusive reality of existence.

To do all this, we have to know something about existence and how it relates to us as knowing subjects. This is crucial for a proper understanding of self-knowledge otherwise we can easily reduce self-knowledge into a knowledge of the internal states of our minds and end up in a kind of solipsism from which we can never get out. Before going any further, however, we should remember that one of the key premises of classical Islamic philosophy was the idea that different modes of existence require different modes of knowledge. By the same token, different modes of knowledge correspond to different modes of existence. This implies that all epistemic claims must clarify what aspect of reality it tries to grasp. Otherwise, we easily confuse between different realms of reality and explain something in terms that are not proper to it. When we talk about knowing existence, we have to know what it implies for our subjectivity.

As we all know, we can give neither a logical definition (*hadd*) nor a description (*taswir*) of existence.[49] A logical definition is based on genus (*jinns*) and specific differentia (*fasl*). In the definition of man as rational animal, for instance, we refer to man's genus "animal" (*hayawan*) and his differentia "rational" (*natiq*). Since definitions apply to classes and not to individuals, a genus designates the general category to which "man" belongs and differentia refers to his specific attributes which distinguish him from the other members of the category of "animal". This, however, does not apply to existence because it has no genus or differentia. To have a genus and/or differentia means to include something and exclude others. To be an "animal" means to exclude the possibility of being a stone or star. But as we intuitively know, there is nothing outside existence, and as the ground of all there is, existence does not leave anything out. It is thus concluded that "since existence is the most general and inclusive of all things, it has no genus, no differentia and no definition".[50]

In a similar way, existence cannot be described for description is based on more evident concepts and definitions than the terms we use for definition. But as the classical philosophers insist, there is no term or concept known to be more evident and clear than existence despite the fact that we may not always able to articulate it in such definitive terms. This suggests that existence can be explained only by itself. But this is a *petitio principi* and not a definition because defining something by itself begs the question. In short, existence is the most evident of all concepts. This conclusion, however, is misleading if not totally wrong because it construes existence as a concept rather than a reality *in concreto*. Our initial assumption was that existence is the ground of all realities including forms of perception and cognition. We then have to conclude that the only proper access to the reality of existence is "illuminative presence" (*hudur ishraqi*) and "essential testimony" (*shuhud ayni*).[51]

This is also based on another premise of classical philosophy, and it is the intrinsic intelligibility of existence. In sharp contrast to the modern concept of existence which is thought to be a variable of entities, existence contains the seeds of meaning and value in itself. It is clear that as the ground of all there is, existence must also be the source of the terms of meaning and intelligibility. Otherwise, reality would be reduced to mere entities with no meaning and life in them. But we know both intuitively and philosophically that this is not the case. The world does not cease to exist as a meaningful structure when I turn my gaze away from it.

Now, the self-intelligibility of existence grants us, the knowing subjects, a position radically different from the modern concepts of the self. In knowing things, we respond to a reality larger than us, and that the moment of encountering an aspect of existence is when meanings emerge as our gateways into reality. This means that the knowing subject cannot claim to be the sole proprietor of meaning and intelligibility, whether it relates to ourselves or to the world around us. The self interprets the world but cannot create it. It has an internal life but cannot claim to be completely disengaged from the world around it. It can turn upon itself but cannot ignore the larger context of reality of which it is a part.

Existence and the Self

In short, we cannot conceive a self without placing it within the larger context of existence. To speak of a self is to speak of relations and contexts of experience within which the self is located. When we talk about the self, we also talk about the non-self, i.e., all that is separate from the self but intimately related to it. In its most basic and simple doing, the self requires and operates within a context of relations and experience. In looking at the tree in front of me, I depend on the intelligibility of the visual experience of the tree: its being before me, my ability to give it a name, its lending itself to be included in my linguistic space, and so on. Any consideration of the self and our ability to know it is made possible by a host of other factors which we call the non-self.

All of these give us a notion of the self that is engaged in the various modalities of existence.

The self does not stand over against a world devoid of meaning, intelligibility and internal relations and then comes to have a primarily cognitive relationship with it. The "engaged self", to use Charles Taylor's suggestive term, is part of the larger context of existence. Since this self is primarily embedded within a larger framework of existence and consciousness, it avoids the dangers of subjectivism. I use the word "subjectivism" not in the sense of arbitrariness or lack of objective standards but in the sense of the self-referential claim of the knowing subject over against the world. Subjectivism implies the closure of the subject upon itself and, by derivation, against the non-subjective and the "supraindividual"[52] This meaning of subjectivism is evident in the disengaged agent of modern philosophy. The modern concept of the self is conceived to be an agent disengaged from any context of relations whether these relations are attributed to the world, things, other human beings, language or existence. The modern self is a worldless subject set against a subject-less world. It is a worldless subject because it is thought to be cut off from all contexts of relation, having a god-like position over the world. It is set against a subject-less world because the world is conceived to be an aggregate of entities that have meaning only when the knowing subject confers upon it some or any meaning. Such a self knows itself and the world around it through a self-professed mastery over the world.

Descartes' *cogito* as an abstract substance set against the *res extensa* is emblematic of disengaged agency for it conceives the self as standing outside the world. Shorn of any existential relations with the non-subjective world except through self-cognition, the Cartesian self takes an "objective" stand towards things and construes them as "objects".[53] Hobbes, perhaps the most important representative of this kind of subjectivism in the seventeenth century, explains the meaning of objectivity as "subject-less world" by saying that "these words of good, evil, and contemptible are ever used with relation to the person that useth them; there being nothing simply or absolutely so, nor any common rule of good and evil to be taken from the nature of the objects themselves but from the person of the man (where there is no commonwealth), or (in a commonwealth) from the person that representeth it".[54]

Once the world is constructed as a cluster of objects whose only reality is summed up in what Galileo called the primary qualities, this "world-less subject"[55] turns to the world and confers meaning upon it. The disengaged self can thus stand outside the world and any context of relations. In this picture, the self not only stands outside the world but also functions as the ontological basis for any notion of intelligibility we may attach to the non-subjective world. By "ontologising" the rational procedures of the mind, the disengaged self of modern subjectivism becomes the sole window to the ontological structure of things and determines the ways in which we encounter the non-subjective world.[56]

This view of the self inevitably leads to what Thomas Nagel calls the "view from nowhere", i.e., the attempt to locate the self in a "no-where" position from which it can look over things while it itself remains essentially untainted by their contingencies.[57] In its modern context, such a notion of the self easily conjures up an imagery of mastery and domination over the world. This is in fact what transpired in the wake of the seventeenth-century Scientific Revolution with the emergence of the modern secular view of the natural environment. Cut off from any context of intelligibility or the so-called secondary qualities, the world of nature came to be seen as an aggregate of dead matter and aimless objects.[58]

In a similar way, the eighteenth-century thought sought to explain knowledge by reducing all terms of object and subject into the internal procedures of the mind. Within this framework, "the nature of human knowledge can only be explained in terms of the ideas which the mind finds within itself".[59] Both the rationalist and empiricist philosophers, seemingly opposed to one another, were in agreement on this fundamental point: all philosophy must start with an analysis of the internal ideas of the mind. This means that one has to turn inside to be able to explain the outside. Paradoxically, the main thrust of modern philosophy seems to agree with the millennium-old dictum of pre-modern philosophy to train the soul so that it can receive the truth. Yet the fundamental difference between the two enterprises is not difficult to see. While traditional philosophy defined the self within a context of intelligibility larger than the self, modern philosophy made it the anchor point of all value and meaning. The traditional self acted with a sense of humility when it turned inward and gazed upon itself because it always saw something more than itself. By contrast, the modern self sees no limits in its self-proclaimed ability to define and determine things, thus leading to a huge sense of hubris and epistemic hegemony.

The Self as a Social Construction

The self as a disengaged agent had its detractors in the twentieth century. The most important criticism has come in the form of constructing the self as a social process. Many social sciences tend to see the self as nothing more than an epiphany of the social conditions within which the self emerges. No figure illustrates this radical interpretation of the self better than Michel Foucault. Through his masterful analyses of power relations, Foucault rejected the Cartesian notion of the self as a disengaged agent. Instead, he proposed to look at the individual through the prism of power mechanisms. For him, the individual emerges within such power relations and cannot escape them.

While Foucault's analysis offers valuable insights into the violent and oppressive nature of modern societies, it moves from one extreme to the other and reduces all agency to a power game. Furthermore, it establishes a tyranny of the social and refuses to recognise any space of freedom for the individual. The Cartesian dichotomy between subject and world is now replaced with a dichotomy between the self and the social.

Foucault and others have a point about the social. When we say "social" today, we refer to an impersonal reality, a reality that is made out of individuals but which has hardly any affinity and intimacy with them. Yet we need not begin again with such a dichotomy. The non-self includes the community at the social level. I prefer the word "community" over "social" as it conveys a more consolidated sense of loyalty, trust and commitment, which lie at the heart of all forms of communal life. The atomistic individual of the modern world undermines the very possibility of creating and sustaining such a community. Many of our social ills result from our failure to understand this point. Our social and communal problems cannot be solved by state regulations alone. We have to change the way we think about the self and the way we relate to the community which is or should always be more than just an aggregate of its members.

Knowing the Self and Beyond

So far, I have spoken about the ways we know and the ways we can talk about the self. I have argued that knowledge is intimately related to existence and all cognition is grounded in an experience, encounter and unveiling of existence and its modalities. Such a concept of knowledge takes us beyond the limits of the various forms of modern subjectivism, which anchors all meaning and intelligibility in the knowing subject. I have also spoken about the self and said that the self by definition implies the existence of the non-self. I made these remarks to show that knowing oneself is neither an act of solipsism and subjectivism nor an act of radical humanism. No matter how we define it, it is an act of encounter, discovery and unveiling.

Now I would like to look at these two terms together and say something about the act of knowing oneself. When we claim to have self-knowledge, we are engaged in a two-fold act. First, we move inward and discover our own inner world. We hold an internal conversation with ourselves, and all of our faculties, i.e., our mind, intellect, heart, spirit, emotions and everything else, participate in this conversation. It is the most personal and intimate encounter we may ever have with any thing. In this sense, trying to know ourselves is a noble act. But as we all know, it is not an easy thing. Goethe once said: "Know thyself? If I knew myself, I would run away!"

Secondly, we move outward and discover that my agency in the world is conditional on the presence of many other things outside me. I cannot ignore their existence, nor should I. I also realise that in contrast to the model of disengagement, engagement entails finitude. Not just *my* self but the self as such is finite and limited in its dealings with things and cannot claim mastery over the world. To have a meaningful life, I have to make peace with them as well as with myself. Turning inward does not cut me off from the world around me. It gives me a new perspective and a broader vision. I can learn to move gracefully between the two realms of reality. I can work through what is called the "anthropocosmic vision", a vision that establishes an essential relationship between the *anthropos* that knows and the *cosmos* that is known.[60]

Knowing the self is thus knowing the cosmos because the self as the microcosmos is a mirror image of the universe as the macrocosmos. This explains why, for instance, Mulla Sadra's use of an anthropomorphic language with reference to the universe does not result in subjectivism or idealism of any kind. Sadra uses the expressions "great man" for the universe and "small universe" for man interchangeably and even says that "man is the totality of all beings as if he is the summa of everything that is in the universe from the species to the genus in terms of [his] capacity and potency".[61] The isomorphic relation that Sadra establishes between man and the universe is clearly articulated in this view and signifies a shared world of intelligibility between the two domains of reality.[62] This approach, however, does not warrant any kind of 'humanism' and man-centeredness because Sadra hastens to add that "the perfections of things are not found in a complete manner except in the True being the Exalted (*haqq al-bari*)".

But to reach this state of equilibrium, I have to be myself first. Being myself here does not mean expanding my individuality to the world or recasting the world around a self-centered epistemology. It means seeing myself within the larger context of existence that surrounds me. It is also a way of seeing myself in relation to God. By having a knowledge of myself, I enter the depths of my inner life and reach the furthest limits of the universe. In both cases, I encounter the Divine as near and far, immanent and transcendent.

Being oneself requires one to be present. Without presence, we live our lives in absentia. In fact, we cannot even call it our lives because it belongs to other moments and eventually to others. Now, one of the definitions of knowledge in the School of Illumination is the presence of an intelligible being to itself. To know is to be in the presence of that which is known. This presence is intellectual, not in the sense of mental approximation but in the sense of participating in the intelligible reality of what I know. This implies a concept of knowledge where we know by removing the veils, i.e., the epistemic obstacles between us and our object of knowledge. In this sense, true knowledge is based on the presence of the knower and the known. To be able to know, I have to be present.

But we all know that to be present is a daunting task. Especially in our world of fast communications, we have lost this sense of presence. We take pride in the fact that we can always be somewhere else mentally, imaginatively and physically. We have all the modern means to destroy all presence from our lives.

This is where self-knowledge comes to our aid as a moment of reflection and introspection. To know oneself is to know what kind of a being we are and what kind of a person we want to be. It is to make a moral scrutiny of ourselves and to arrive at making some ethical choices. In this sense, knowing oneself is a deeply practical act because it is a reflection upon our state of existence and what we want to do with it. This is what Heidegger has called "authentic existence". The condition of authenticity is the self's ability to know who he/she is: It is to resist the temptations of the inner and outer worlds without declaring either one of them our enemy.

Heidegger's model of authenticity, however, falls short of setting any moral standards by which we can authenticate ourselves. Knowing oneself is a deeply moral act because its goal is not to produce another epistemic statement but orient my existence towards a structure of meaning. As Socrates explains in the *Phaedrus*, his main reason for seeking the knowledge of his own self is to learn how to lead a morally right life. This is where philosophy becomes a spiritual exercise and goes beyond analytical bickering. This goal can be achieved by placing the self within a "whole", which is the cosmos, and within an ontological proximity to the Ideas. A self or soul not nourished by the Truth is at a loss. Yet it can recover itself from such a fall by self-introspection and "recollection" (*anamnesis*).[63] Socrates' concern to establish self-knowledge as a guide for moral life has much in common with the Islamic philosophical tradition and its attempt to recast knowledge as a simultaneous experience in ontology and spirituality. This is clearly found in a saying attributed to the Prophet of Islam: "He who [who he] has known his self/soul has known his Lord" (*man 'arafa nafsahu faqad 'arafa rabbahu*).

One knows the self only to discover that it is more than my individual thoughts, wishes, desires, etc. It is intimately connected with the Divine for it is here in our own selves that we gain the certainty about ourselves, the world and God – not in some laboratory or lecture hall. This relationship between the self and the non-self forces the self to be more than what it is. The self gains meaning and becomes fulfilled when it is no longer just itself. It is bound to rise above itself to realise its full potential to be the receptacle of the breath of the Compassionate and vicegerent on earth. Leth unto itself, the self, just like reason, is self-destructive, and we need little evidence to prove this when we look at history.

In conclusion, the self, in order to reach a higher state of consciousness, must connect with a higher realm of reality. Connecting with that reality requires intellectual clarity, spiritual refinement and moral rectitude, all of which are ways of participating in the truth. Let me finish with a quote from Mulla Sadra who, like Ibn al-'Arabi, saw the salvation of the self in its intellectual rigor and spiritual fulfillment:

One of the aspects of being human is [his ability] to represent universal meanings completely disembodied from matter as explained in discussions of the intellect, the intelligible and other related subjects. Arriving at the knowledge of the unknown is through definition and description on the basis of what is presently known. The most special kind of this knowledge is the conjunction of certain human souls with the Divine world in such a way that it becomes extinct from its own essence and subsists with the subsistence [of the Divine world]. This way, the True One becomes his ear, eye, hand, and foot. And this is assuming the characteristics of God the Exalted.[64]

Conclusion: Is Return to Reason Still Possible?

As I have argued so far, rationality as intelligibility moves us beyond the internal workings of a single, disengaged mind and places us within a larger context of ontological significance. The metaphysics of creation establishes the Quranic notion of substantive rationality derived from the intrinsic intelligibility of the realm of existence. Knowledge as the disclosure of the inherent order and structure of things rejects instrumentalist and subjectivist rationality and instead sets up a context of intelligibility in which our reason and thinking function as a response to the call of reality. The ontological ground of reason enables it to participate in the intelligible order of existence and thus makes it a situated and contextualised reality. Furthermore, reason is also an inter-subjective principle and does not function in a solipsistic environment.

As a book of revelation and guidance, the Quran treats human reason and thinking in this larger context of the created order of existence. While having full confidence in uncorrupted reason, it warns against ontological reductionism, epistemological hubris and moral egotism. Reason is a God-given gift with which we access the reality of things. But it is unreasonable to claim that reason alone can give us meaning and freedom. One also needs spiritual guidance through which reason is to be illuminated. The heart as our deep conscience guarantees that procedural rationality, which we employ in our daily dealings, does not trump other types of reasoning and thinking. Reason nourished by faith gains a deeper insight into the reality of things because it can set its own limits and finds its proper place in the "circle of existence" (*da'irat al-wujud*). Faith articulated by reason and communicated through language can bring about certainty (*al-yaqin*), which the Quran deems essential for our mental and spiritual integrity. (Al-An'am, 6:75; Al-Takathur, 102:5–7).

Recovering the Quranic path of thinking and the traditional meaning of '*aql* is an urgent task for the contemporary Muslim world. This is a task that extends to such diverse fields as law, education, art, science and politics and certainly not limited to the interests and aspirations of Muslim nations alone. The erosion of the principle of reason in late modernity has hurt human aspirations globally to create a world based on reason, justice and equality. The vacuum created by the failure of the Enlightenment reason has been filled with the new forces of global hyper-capitalism, culture of nihilism and narcissism, and scientistic hubris. As the main terms of reference of the new global order, productivity, profit and efficiency now define what it means to live a rational life both individually and communally. The current world order creates new definitions of rationality and reasonableness through an increasingly sophisticated system of public discourse, mass education, technological innovation, instant communication and the hourly creation of countless virtual worlds, all of which give the appearance that our search for meaning has ended and that we as rational and free human beings have finally created a purely human world free from unjustified beliefs and transcendent illusions.

Philosophically speaking, the inherent contradiction of rationalism is that it assumes its own ontological ground and reproduces reality in such a way as to justify a self-referential notion of human reason. Neither reality nor reason, however, warrants a self-grounding reason. Reason by nature and function operates with terms and tools both within and outside itself. As a principle of 'tying together', 'gathering' and 'protecting', reason always reaches out beyond itself and connects us with the larger reality of existence and human language. Pure rationalism ends up in radical solipsism and thus contradicts reason.

Reason as a self-grounded principle cannot move us beyond the current state of humanity; it only reinforces and reproduces its metaphysical fallacies. A humanity so deeply enclosed upon itself to be the master of the universe while not taking the moral responsibility that comes with such a claim has created a world in which the principle of reason has disappeared, subjective consciousness has been absolutized, and a profound alienation between the human person and his work has set in. The more we reduce everything to utility and maximize the use-value of whatever happens to be around us, the more we lose the chance to retain the meaning of logos as connecting different orders of reality and protecting ourselves from error.

A new concept of reason is thus needed to recover the meaning of the human person as a 'being who thinks' (*haywan natiq*), i.e., who sees, hears, listens, encounters, responds, reacts, contemplates, and engages in other acts of human intelligence and will and never loses sight of the larger reality of which he/she is a part. Such a recovery is possible but it requires a re-assessment of the key notions and values with which we operate today. Reason as tying together, connecting and protecting will re-emerge only when we remember that reason is not about the human person or his interests or even his reasoning but rather about existence and beings, their meaning, relations and connections, and about the ways in which we respond to the call of reality.

> *Say: [Know] then, that the final evidence [of all truth] rests with God alone. {149} (Al-An'am, 6:149).*

Endnotes

1. Cf. Milton K. Munitz, *The Question of Reality* (Princeton: Princeton University Press, 1990), p. 124.
2. See my "Roots of Misconception: Euro-American Perceptions of Islam Before and After September 11th" in *Islam, Fundamentalism, and the Betrayal of Tradition*, Joseph Lumbard (ed.) (Bloomington, IN: World Wisdom, 2009, 2nd edition), pp. 149–193.
3. Kant, "What is Enlightenment?" in *Kant on History*, ed. Lewis White Beck, (New York: Macmillan Publishing Company, 1963), p. 3.
4. Louis Dupre, *The Enlightenment and the Intellectual Foundations of Modern Culture* (New Haven and London: Yale University Press, 2004), Preface, ix.
5. Ayn Rand, *The Virtue of Selfishness* (New American Library 1964) p. 25.
6. For a view of modernity as control and predictibility, see Albert Borgmann, *Crossing the Postmodern Divide* (Chicago: fte University of Chicago Press, 1992).

7. Cf. Charles Taylor, "Rationality" in his *Philosophy and the Human Sciences,* Volume 2 (Cambridge: Cambridge University Press, 1985), p. 134.

8. Heidegger rejects this impowerished meaning of 'logos' as 'discourse' or 'analysis' without an ontological ground. Instead, he tries to recover the original Greek meaning of logos as 'gathering' and 'togetherness'. See his *An Introduction to Metaphysics,* tr. R. Manheim, (New Haven and London: Yale University Press, 1959), pp. 120–135.

9. Paul Feyerabend, who in his *Against the Method* (1975) took upon himself to debunk the absolutist claims of positivist science, is prob- ably the most famous proponent of the second view. Richard Rorty's *Philosophy and the Mirror of Nature* (1979) provides another constructivist critique of the Enlightenment project of pure reason. Rorty's alternative is a sort of reason dissolved into human drama. For a discussion of the trails of modern reason in Western philosophy in the 20th century, see Stephen Toulmin, *Return to Reason* (Cambridge: Harvard University Press, 2001).

10. See Denys Turner, *Faith, Reason and the Existence of God* (Cambridge: Cambridge University Press, 2004), especially pp. 75–88.

11. Mulla Sadra, *al-Hikmat al-muta'aliyah f i'l-asf ar al-'aqliyyat al-arba'ah*, (Beirut: Dar Ihya' al-Turath al-'Arabi, 1981) I, 2, p. 315. Sadra goes on to say: "the difference between the sciences based on theory and the sciences based on vision, is like the difference between someone who knows the definition of sweetness and someone who has actually tasted sweetness; and someone who understands the definition of health and power and someone who is actually healthy and powerful." Commentary on the Chapter al-Waqi'ah, Tafsir, Vol. 7, p. 10. For more on this, see my *Knowledge in Later*

Islamic Philosophy: Mulla Sadra On Existence, Intellect and Intuition, (New York: Oxford University Press, 2010), pp. 217–221.

12. What Kant has to say about this is worth quoting in full: “If reason will not subject itself to the law it gives itself, it will have to bow under the yoke of the law which others impose on it, for without any law what- soever nothing, not even the greatest nonsense, can play its hand for very long. ftus the inevitable consequence of declared lawlessness in thinking (an emancipation from restrictions of reason) is that freedom to think is finally lost.” Kant, “What is Orientation in thinking?”, trans. L. W. Beck in *Kant’s Critique of Practical Reason and Other Writings on Moral Philosophy* (Chicago, 1949), p. 304.

13. Kant, *The Critique of Pure Reason,* trans. Norman Kemp Smith (Lon- don, 1933), p. A viii.

14. Cf. Fazlur Rahman, *Major Themes of the Quran* (Minneapolis: Bibliotheca Islamica, 1994), p. 22.

15. Harith al-Muhasibi, *Sharaf al-‘aql wa mahiyyatuhu,* ed. M. A. ‘Ata (Beirut: Dar al-Kutub al-‘Ilmiyyah), 1982, p. 19.

16. Haydar Amuli, *Jami’ al-esrar wa manba’ al-anwar,* ed. By Henry Corbin and Osman Yahia (Tehran: Department d’iranologie de l’institut franco-iranien de recherche, 1968), pp. 372–3.

17. Raghib al-Isfahani, *al-Mufradat fi gharib al-Quran* (Istanbul: Kahraman Yayinlari, 1986), p. 511. Both Harith al-Muhasibi and al-Ghazali refer to this two-fold definition of reason; see al-Muhasibi, *Sharaf al-‘aql,* p. 20.

18. Al-Farabi identifies this as one of the six meanings of *‘aql;* see al-Fararabi, *Risalah fi’l-‘aql,* ed. Maurice Bouyges (Beyrouth, Lebanon: Dar el-Machreq, 1983), pp. 8–9.

19. The later philosophical tradition has developed an elaborate epistemology and anthropology of reason which includes *'aql hayulani* or *'aql bi'l-quwwah,* the material or potential intellect, *'aql bi'l-fi'l,* the actualised intellect, *'aql mustafad,* the acquired intellect, and finally *'aql fa''al,* the active intellect. Since I cannot discuss these later interpretations here, I will only refer to the foundational texts by the philosophers. For al- Kindi's discussion and classification of *'aql,* which is the first among the philosophers, see his *Risalah fi'l-'aql* ('On the Intellect'), ed. Jean Jolivet in *L'Intellect selon Kindi* (Leiden, Holland: E. J. Brill, 1971). Al-Farabi fully develops al-Kindi's initial exploration in his various works; see especially Risalah fi'l-*'aql.* Ibn Sina discusses *'aql* and its types and functions in his various works including the *Shifa'* and *Najat* but also *al-Mabda' wa'l-ma'ad.* For an extensive survey of their views against the Greek back- ground, see Davidson, Herbert A., *al-Farabi, Avicenna, and Averroes on Intel- lect: Their Cosmologies, Theories of the Active Intellect, and Theories of Human Intellect* (New York/Oxford: Oxford University Press, 1992).

20. Mulla Sadra, *Risālat al-h. ashr,* ed. with Persian translation by M. Khwājawī (Tehran: Intishārāt-i Mawlawī, 1998), pp. 85–6.

21. Ibn al-Manzur, *Lisan al-'Arab,* entries on '*aql* and *qulb* (Beirut: no date) Vol. I. p. 687 and Vol. XI, pp. 458–9.

22. Abu Hayyan al-Tawhidi, *al-Muqabasat,* ed. H. Sandubo (Tunisia: Dar al-Ma'arif, 1991), p. 7.

23. Compare this with what Zarathustra says to the people who show no interest in what he has to say: "Must one first shatter their ears to teach them to hear with their eyes?", F. Nietzsche, *Thus Spoke Zarathustra,* tr. R. J. Hollingdale (Middlesex: Penguin Books, 1961), p. 45.

24. Al-Ghazali, *Rawdat al-talibin wa 'umdat al-salikin, in Majmu'ah Rasa'il al-Imam al-Ghazali* (Beirut: Dar al-Kutub al-'Ilmiyyah, 1994), p. 32.

25. Ibn Kathir, *Tafsir al-Quran al-'azim,* (Beirut: Dar al-Ma'rifah, 2006), p. 1141.

26. Ibn Kathir, *Tafsir*, p. 659.

27. Cf. Martin Heidegger, *What is Called Thinking?,* tr. J. G. Gray (New York: Harper Books, 1968), p. 165.

28. Abu 'Abdallah Muhammad ibn 'Ali al-Hakim al-Tirmidhi, *Bayan al-farq bayn al-sadr wa'l-qalb wa'l-fu'ad wa'l-lubb,* (Amman: al-Markaz al-Maliki li'l-Buhuth wa'l-Dirasat al-Islamiyyah, 2009), p. 15. For the English translation of al-Tirmidhi's work see Nicholas Heer, trans., "A Treatise on the Heart," in *Three Early Sufi Texts*, trans. Nicholas Heer et al., Revised Edition (Louisville, KY: Fons Vitae, 2009).

29. This evocative phrase by Shah Waliullah of Delhi (d. 1762), one of the greatest scholars of the sub-continent of India, also sums up the integrative approach of classical Muslim thinkers towards the human person. See his *Hujjat al-Allah Balighah* (Cairo: Dar al-Turath, nd.), Vol. II, p. 89.

30. This premise is also the basis of the argument that this is the best of all possible worlds which God could create. For this version of the "ahsan al-nizam" argument, see my "Mulla Sadra on Theodicy and the Best of All Possible Worlds", *Oxford Journal of Islamic Studies*, 18:2 (2007), pp. 183–201.

31. Muhammad 'Ali al-Tahanawi, *Kashshaf istilahat al-funun* (Beirut: Dar al-Kutub al-'Ilmiyyah), Vol. 3, *Kashshaf*, III, p. 307.

32. Toshihiko Izutsu, *God and Man in the Quran: The Semantics of the Koranic Weltanschauung* (Tokyo: The Keio Institute of

Cultural and Linguistic Studies, 1964), pp. 136-7.

33. Ibn Kathir, *Tafsir* , p. 334.

34. Abu Abdallah al-Qurtubi, *al-Jami' li-ahkam al-Quran* (Beirut: Dar Ibn Hazm, 2004), Vol I, p. 780.

35. This and similar verses underlie the commonly held view in the Islamic tradition that the entire universe is alive and that "everything has soul". See Ibn Kathir, Tafsir, p. 932. Mulla Sadra holds that "all animal, plant and inanimate natures have knowledge and consciousness by themselves, through the necessities of their essences, and their particular effects on account of their partaking of existence because existence is identical with light and manifestation. Existence is therefore united with the qualities of the perfection of existence in knowledge, power, volition, life, and the like." *Ajwibat al-masa'il al-kashaniyyah in Majmu'a- yi rasa'il-i falsafi-yi Sadr al-Muta'allihin,* ed. Hamid Naji Isfahani (Tehran: Intisharat-i Hikmat, AH 1375), p. 137. For more on the ontological vitalism of Islamic cosmology, see my *Knowledge in Later Islamic Philosophy,* pp. 229-32.

36. Quoting a popular saying, Tahanawi describes it as follows: "God has mounted reason in the angels without carnal desire, put desires in the animals without reason, and in the children of Adam both of them. ftus whoever has his reason triumph over his carnal desires, he is better than the angels, and whoever has his carnal desires triumph over his reason, he is lower than the animals". Tahanawi, *Kashshaf,* Vol. 3, p. 314.

37. Isfahani, *al-Mufradat,* p. 833

38. Tahanawi, *Kashshaf,* Vol. 3, p. 314.

39. Ibn Miskawayh, *The Refinement of Character (Tahdhib al-akhlaq),* tr. Constantine K. Zurayk (Beirut: fte American

University of Beirut, 1968), p. 106.

40. Ibn Hazm, *al-Ahklaq wa'l-siyar fi mudawat al-nufus,* ed. Tahir Ahmad Makki (Jeddah: Dar al-Manarah, 2007), p. 124.

41. Ibn Miskawayh, *The Refinement of Character,* p. 44. Ibn Miskawayh goes on to say that "the proper food of the rational soul is knowledge, the acquisition of intelligibles, the practice of veracity in one's opinions, the acceptance of truth no matter where or with whom it may be, and the shunning of falsehood and lying whatever it may be or whence it may come".

42. Werner Heisenberg, *Physics and Philosophy: The Revolution in Modern Science* (New York: Harper and Row Publishers, 1958), p. 2.

43. *Mysticism and Logic* (New York: Doubleday Anchor Books, 1957), p. 45.

44. John Searle, *The Rediscovery of Mind* (Cambridge, MA: Massachusetts Institute of Technology Press, 1994), p. 30.

45. Seyyed Hossein Nasr has dealt with this issue in many of his writings. See my "The Sacred versus the Secular: Nasr on Science", *Library of Living Philosophers: Seyyed Hossein Nasr,* ed. L. E. Hahn, R. E. Auxier and L. W. Stone (Chicago: Open Court Press, 2001), pp. 445-462. See also Muzaffar Iqbal, *Islam and Science* (Ashgate, 2002).

46. For a detailed analysis of the three major views of science represented by these figures in the Islamic world, see my "Three Views of Science in the Islamic World" in *God, Life and the Cosmos: Christian and Islamic Perspectives,* eds. Ted Peters, Muzaffar Iqbal, Syed Nomanul Haq, (Ashgate, 2002), pp. 43-75.

47. Plato, Protagoras 343-ab, Alcibiades 129a.

48. Joseph J. Kockelmans, "Some Fundamental Themes of

Husserl's Phenomenology" in Phenomenology: *The Philosophy of Edmund Husserl and Its Interpretation,* edited by Joseph J. Kockelmans (New York: Anchor Books, 1967), p. 36.

49. *Asfar*, I, 1, p. 25.

50. Ibid.

51. *Kitab al-Masha'ir*, p. 24. Sadra adds that "knowledge about existence can be acquired either by seeing by presence (*al-mushahadah al-huduriyyah*) or through rational argumentation by analyzing its effects (i.e. its appear- ances) and concomitants, but this kind of knowledge obtained through reasoning is no other than a flimsy knowledge". *Asfar*, p. 53.

52. Charles Taylor, "What is Human Agency?", in his *Human Agency and Language: Philosophical Papers 1* (Cambridge: Cambridge University Press, 1999), pp. 15–44 and ibidem., "Lichtung or Lebensform: Parallels Between Heidegger and Wittgenstein" in his *Philosophical Arguments* (Cambridge, MA: Harvard University Press, 1995), pp. 61–78.

53. Historically speaking, the ontological closure of the knowing subject unto itself was a crucial step towards the secularisation of knowledge: a knowledge that is closed upon itself ought to work from within itself with- out being in need of a supra-individual and transcendent principle. It is not accidental that Descartes' cogito came to mark the beginning of a secular and 'free' knowledge, first free from Scholastic philosophy and then from any other supra-individual principle in a manner that Anthony Flew calls "Protestant individualism secularized". See his *An Introduction to Western Philosophy* (New York: Thames and Hudson, 1989), p. 280; cf. also pp. 78–90.

54. Leviathan, Chapter VI, in Britannica Great Books (Chicago: Encyclo- pedia Britannica, Inc., 1952), Vol. 23, pp. 61–2.

55. Guignon, op. cit., p. 98.

56. Charles Taylor, "Engaged Agency and Background in Heidegger" in *The Cambridge Companion to Heidegger*, edited by Charles B. Guignon (Cambridge: Cambridge University Press, 1993), p. 317.

57. Thomas Nagel, *Mortal Questions* (Cambridge: Cambridge University Press, 1979), p. 4. See also his *The View From Nowhere* (New York: Oxford University Press, 1986).

58. For the historical importance and critique of Galileo's distinction between the primary and secondary qualities, see, inter alia, R.G. Colling- wood, *The Idea of Nature* (Oxford: Oxford University Press, 1945), pp. 102–5; Wolfgang Smith, *Cosmos and Transcendence Breaking Through the Barrier of Scientistic Belief* (Illinois: Sherwood Sugden & Company, 1984), pp. 15–16; Alexander Koyre, *From the Closed World to the Infinite Universe* (Baltimore: The Johns Hopkins University Press, 1957), pp. 88–109; S.H. Nasr, *Religion and the Order of Nature* (Oxford: Oxford University Press, 1996), pp. 136–8; Ian Barbour, *Religion and Science Historical and Contemporary Issues* (San Francisco: Harper SanFrancisco, 1997), pp. 9–17; E. Burtt, *The Metaphysical Foundations of Modern Physical Science* (New York: Doubleday Anchor Books, 1932), pp. 83–91.

59. Ernest Cassirer, *The Philosophy of the Enlightenment* (Princeton: Princeton University Press, 1979), p. 94.

60. William C. Chittick, *The Heart of Islamic Philosophy* (Oxford University Press, 2001), p. 65.

61. *Asfar*, III, 2, p. 180. See also the following: "Man is the microcosm (*'alam saghir*) comprised of three stages: the highest is the soul and the lowest is the body together with sound mixture, which is the blood, and the middle is the spirit." *Asfar*, II, 1, p. 157.

62. It is due to this isomorphic unity that neither skepticism nor the mind-body problem ever became a real issue in Islamic philosophy. For Sadra, as for other traditional philosophers, the ontological reality of the non-subjective world or the objective content of thought is always a given that precedes our discursive-mental constructions of it.

63. Charles L. Griswold, *Self-Knowledge in Plato's Phaedrus* (New Haven and London: Yale University Press, 1986), pp. 2–3.

64. *Asfar*, IV, 2, pp. 81–2.